THE CHILDREN'S
ANIMAL ATLAS

THE CHILDREN'S
ANIMAL ATLAS

**HOW ANIMALS HAVE EVOLVED,
WHERE THEY LIVE TODAY,
WHY SO MANY ARE IN DANGER**

DAVID LAMBERT

The Millbrook Press
Brookfield, Ct.

A QUARTO BOOK

First published in the United States of America in
1992 by
The Millbrook Press Inc.
2 Old New Milford Road
Brookfield, Connecticut 06804.

Library of Congress Cataloging-in-Publication Data

Lambert, David. 1932–
    The children's animal atlas / by David Lambert.
        p.   cm.
    Includes index.
    Summary: Maps and text depict animals and their location on the
Earth, explaining why species live where they do and how they have
evolved to adjust to varied habitats.
    ISBN 1–56294–101–1 (trade ed.).—ISBN 1–56294–167–4 (lib. ed.)
    1. Zoogeography—Maps.   [1. Animal distribution—Maps.]
I. Title.   II. Title: Animal atlas.
G1046.D4L3   1992 <G&M>
591.9′022′3—dc20   91–30147
                                        CIP
                                 MAP AC

This book was designed and produced by
Quarto Publishing plc
6 Blundell Street
London N7 9BH

Publishing Director Janet Slingsby
Art Director Nick Buzzard
Art Editor Anne Fisher
Designer Patrick Knowles
Illustrations Wayne Ford
Maps Janos Marffy
Picture Manager Sarah Risley

The Publishers would like to thank the following for
their help in the preparation of this book: Bob Burns,
Neal Cobourne, Penny Dawes, Stefanie Foster,
Louise Morley, Constance Novis, Jenny Vaughan.

Typeset in Great Britain by Bookworm Typesetting,
Manchester.
Color separations in Singapore by Eray Scan (Pte) Ltd.
Printed in Singapore by Star Standard Industries
(Pte) Ltd.
Library binding in USA by Worzalla Publishing Co.

CONTENTS

The world is home for over a million different kinds of animals — far more than most of us can imagine. They range in size from tiny microscopic creatures to huge whales — with a whole range of other animals in between.

THE FAMILY OF ANIMALS

Scientists divide all living things into different species, or kinds. About 44,000 species of animals are vertebrates, which means they are creatures with a backbone. Of these, there are about 21,000 species of fishes, 8,600 species of birds, and about 6,500 reptiles, such as lizards and snakes. There are about 4,000 species of amphibians (frogs, toads, salamanders, and other animals that mostly live on land and breed in water) and the same number of mammals (warm-blooded creatures, with hair on their bodies).

But these are just a few of the world's animals. The vertebrates are far outnumbered by the invertebrates (animals without a backbone). There are four times as many kinds of snails, slugs, squid, and other mollusks (shelled animals) as fishes. The largest group of all is the insects. About a million kinds have been identified, and scientists think there may be 30 million more species still undiscovered.

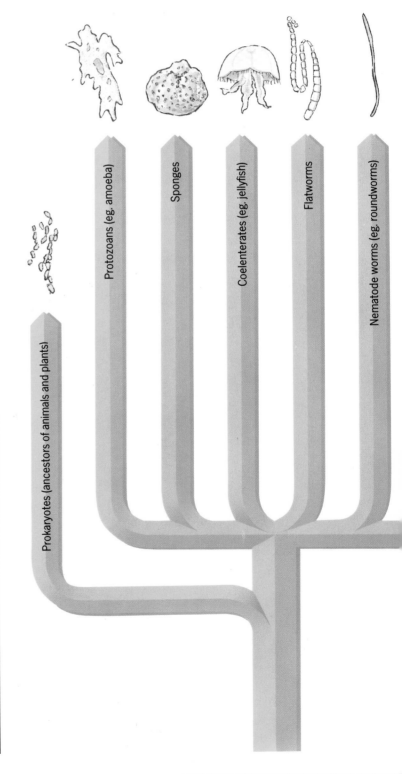

Prokaryotes (ancestors of animals and plants)

Protozoans (eg. amoeba)

Sponges

Coelenterates (eg. jellyfish)

Flatworms

Nematode worms (eg. roundworms)

One-celled organisms

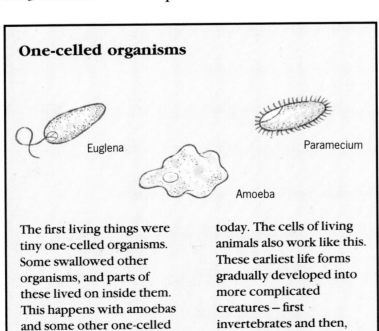

Euglena

Paramecium

Amoeba

The first living things were tiny one-celled organisms. Some swallowed other organisms, and parts of these lived on inside them. This happens with amoebas and some other one-celled organisms that still survive today. The cells of living animals also work like this. These earliest life forms gradually developed into more complicated creatures — first invertebrates and then, eventually, into vertebrates.

Close relations

New species of animals sprang from old ones, when animals of the same kind got separated from each other. This happened to a kind of gull that, long ago, spread around the northern oceans of the world.

Separate groups settled in different places and gradually changed. One gave rise to the herring gull (left) and another to the lesser black-backed gull (right). The birds look alike, but there are important differences. Herring gulls have a gray back and most have pink legs. Lesser black-backed gulls have a darker back and yellow legs.

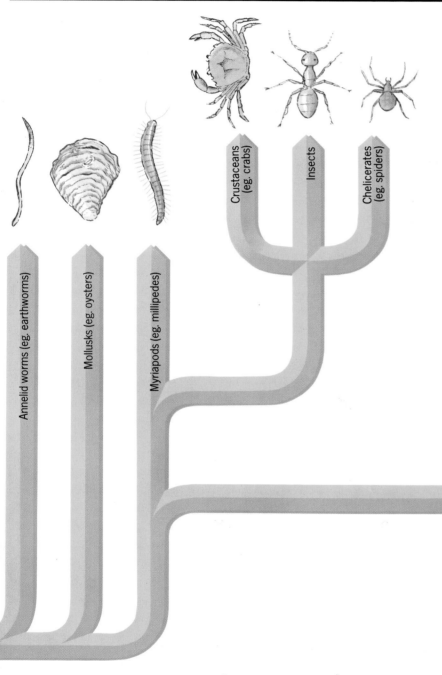

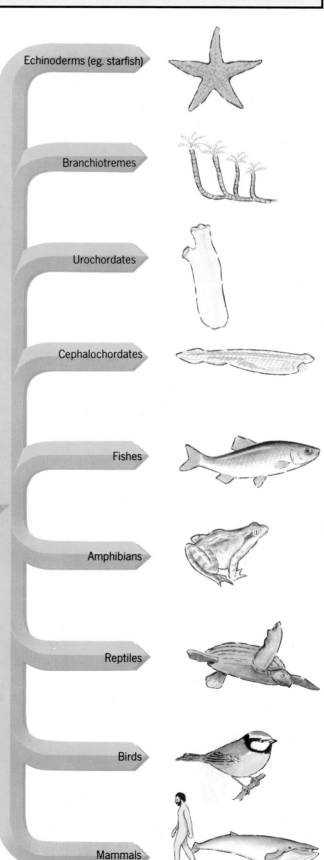

Annelid worms (eg. earthworms)

Mollusks (eg. oysters)

Myriapods (eg. millipedes)

Crustaceans (eg. crabs)

Insects

Chelicerates (eg. spiders)

Echinoderms (eg. starfish)

Branchiotremes

Urochordates

Cephalochordates

Fishes

Amphibians

Reptiles

Birds

Mammals

This 'family tree' shows how most main groups of animals are related. Prokaryotes are tiny relatives of both plants and animals. Protozoans are one-celled organisms. The rest are true animals, with many cells. Sponges live in water, fixed to one place, like plants. Coelenterates include jellyfish. The best-known worms are annelid worms: Earthworms belong to this group.

Snails and oysters are examples of mollusks, while centipedes and millipedes are myriapods. Shrimps and crabs are crustaceans. Ants, bees, and flies are just a few of the many kinds of insects. Scorpions and spiders are chelicerates, and starfish are echinoderms. Branchiotremes, urochordates, and cephalochordates are small sea creatures related to vertebrates.

HOW ANIMALS CHANGE

Very slowly, over the millions of years since life began, living things have changed. Animals that existed in the distant past have developed into new ones, better suited to living in certain ways and places. This process is called evolution and it works like this.

An animal's body is made up of many little cells. Each cell contains tiny units called genes that come from its parents. Genes make sure that young animals grow up like their parents.

Sometimes, one gene changes. Then the young animal becomes slightly different from its parents. If that makes life harder for the animal, it will soon die. But if the change makes it better at surviving than its parents, it will grow up and pass on the new gene to its own young. As these new kinds of animals multiply, their less-successful relatives die out. In time, new genes can produce brand new species of animals. Every kind of animals that swims, walks, climbs, or flies evolved this way.

One way to see how evolution works is to look at life on a lonely island. Volcanic islands may push their way up from the ocean floor. At first, they are quite lifeless. In time, a few animals and plants drift to the islands by chance from the mainland, far away, and are cut off from others like them. Gradually, their descendants become better suited to life on the island. Different species evolve from the first animals to survive, each one able to make the most of the island's food supplies.

Galápagos finches

In the 1830s, the zoologist Charles Darwin visited the remote Galápagos Islands off the west coast of South America. He noticed many kinds of finches. Some had small, slender beaks and ate insects. Others had short, deep beaks for cracking and eating very hard seeds. Yet others, with different beaks, ate a mixture of foods — buds, leaves, or insects. Darwin realized that they were descended from a single kind of finch from the mainland. They had evolved, on the islands, to make the most of different foods. Darwin saw from these finches how one species, or kind, of animal can give rise to many different new kinds.

Dogs from wolves

Wolves (below left) are the early ancestors of modern breeds of dogs. First, hunters probably tamed wolves and let these breed. In each litter, not all cubs were alike. By breeding always from dogs that were unusual in some way, people produced different kinds of working dogs, such as the husky (below center), and breeds such as poodles (below right), which are now kept as pets.

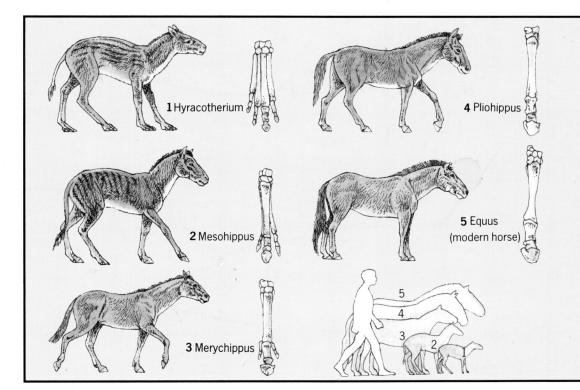

1 Hyracotherium

2 Mesohippus

3 Merychippus

4 Pliohippus

5 Equus
(modern horse)

How horses evolved

The early horse, *Hyracotherium*, was a cat-sized forest dweller. It had four-toed forefeet and three-toed hind feet. It gave rise to larger kinds, such as *Mesohippus* and *Merychippus*, with longer legs and fewer toes. *Merychippus* could run fast and lived on grassy plains, where it could see attackers and run away. From this came the first one-toed horse called *Pliohippus*. About two million years ago, this gave rise to *Equus*, the modern horse.

Right Dark and pale peppered moths on a tree trunk show how nature seems to select animals that can survive the best. Dark moths were once much scarcer than pale ones because the tree bark where they lived was pale. Pale moths were difficult to see against pale bark, but birds easily found and ate most of the dark moths. Then soot from smoky city chimneys darkened the bark. This showed up the pale moths, so most of these were eaten by the birds. Now the dark moths became difficult to see, so these bred and multiplied. Today, clean-air laws have made the tree bark clean again. Once more, birds find and eat most of the dark moths, so these are disappearing, while the pale moths are making a comeback.

Above and right Most animals have to evolve in ways that help them fight enemies and compete with other creatures for food. Animals isolated on remote islands can evolve in different ways. Without predators to keep them in check, some island animals become unusually large. Tortoises, big enough to ride on, lumber around on the Galápagos Islands (above). Lizards like this Komodo dragon, big enough to kill a pig, roam small Indonesian islands (right).

ANIMAL COMMUNITIES

Imagine walking in a woodland. Birds fly from the trees, insects and their larva eat bark and leaves, and tiny animals live among the rotting vegetation at your feet. A forest is home to millions of creatures. Most are so small that you can only see them through a microscope.

Food connects all these animals to each other. Some eat plants and some eat the plant eaters. Droppings and the remains of dead animals fertilize the soil, helping more plants to grow for animals to eat. So food goes around and around in a cycle.

Animals and plants that live together in a place make up a biological community. A community may be small and simple — just the animals that live on a single leaf. A tree holds a much larger community, and a woodland holds an even larger one.

Some kinds of animals make homes, such as nests or burrows. Most do not. They wander around in search of food or a mate, though they usually stay inside a certain kind of habitat, or living place. For example, fish of fast mountain streams do not swim into slow muddy water. Grasshoppers stay in grassy meadows.

Some animals move around in only part of their habitat. This area is called the home range. Home ranges can be huge or tiny. A mouse's might be the corner of a field. An eagle's could cover several mountains and valleys, perhaps overlapping with the home ranges of several other eagles. But, if an eagle strays too far into the home range of another one, it will be driven away.

In the same way, a fox or an ape family keeps others of its own kind out of a special area inside its home range. This defended area is called a territory.

Bird fight

Many animals — such as these great tits (left) — lay claim to a "territory" — an area where they live and breed. A male defends his territory. He and a female raise young and find food there. Many male songbirds sing to show they 'own' territory. Any rival will be threatened. Some birds fight quite fiercely, to drive other males away.

Above A greenfinch feeds its young in their nest. Birds' nests are temporary homes where they can lay their eggs and raise a family.

Below Sea lions make no home, but come ashore to breed. Strong males defend a stretch of beach to stop rivals from stealing their mates.

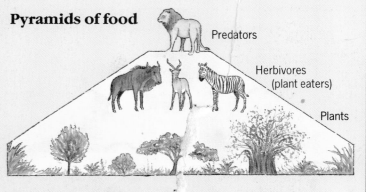

Pyramids of food

Predators

Herbivores (plant eaters)

Plants

In animal communities, food forms a kind of pyramid. A great number of plants feeds a lesser number of herbivores, which feed a smaller number of predators. The diagram shows a food pyramid in East Africa's Serengeti area. The lion forms the tip.

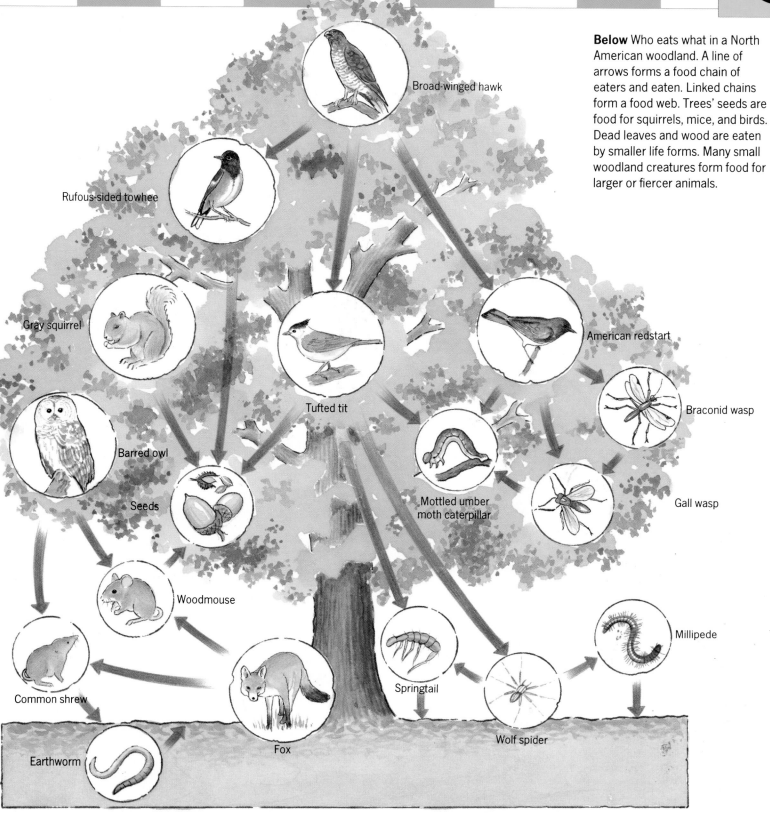

Below Who eats what in a North American woodland. A line of arrows forms a food chain of eaters and eaten. Linked chains form a food web. Trees' seeds are food for squirrels, mice, and birds. Dead leaves and wood are eaten by smaller life forms. Many small woodland creatures form food for larger or fiercer animals.

Broad-winged hawk

Rufous-sided towhee

Gray squirrel

American redstart

Barred owl

Tufted tit

Braconid wasp

Seeds

Mottled umber moth caterpillar

Gall wasp

Woodmouse

Millipede

Common shrew

Springtail

Wolf spider

Earthworm

Fox

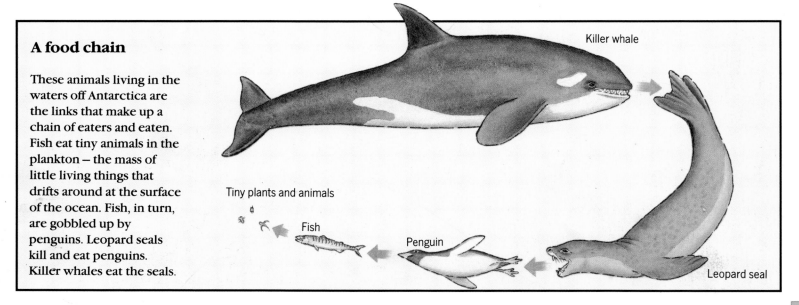

A food chain

These animals living in the waters off Antarctica are the links that make up a chain of eaters and eaten. Fish eat tiny animals in the plankton – the mass of little living things that drifts around at the surface of the ocean. Fish, in turn, are gobbled up by penguins. Leopard seals kill and eat penguins. Killer whales eat the seals.

Killer whale

Tiny plants and animals

Fish

Penguin

Leopard seal

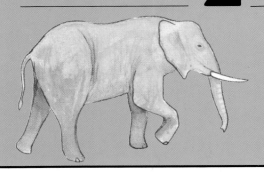

Animals live in many kinds of habitats — some hot, some cold, some wet, and some dry. Most animals can only live in one kind of habitat — they cannot move into a different one and survive. Fish, for example, cannot live for long out of water.

Below This red-eyed tree frog comes from a small island off Panama in Central America. There are many other animals living only in a tiny corner of the world: perhaps in one cave or on one mountainside.

WHERE ANIMALS LIVE

Geographers divide all land into biomes, or life zones. Each biome has a kind of climate that suits only certain types of plants and animals.

The map on this page shows some of these different zones. The tops of high mountains and the Arctic and Antarctic regions of the far north and south are cold lands largely under ice and snow. South of the Arctic, a great belt of cold northern forest runs through North America, Europe, and Asia. Temperate woods filled with broad-leaved trees grow in the milder climates south of this forest. Drier lands include grasslands and deserts. Tropical rain forests thrive in hot, wet areas close to the equator.

Later pages of this book look at the animals that live in these different places.

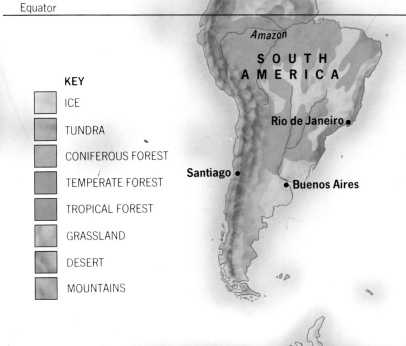

GREENLAND

NORTH AMERICA

Mackenzie

Nelson

Rocky Mountains

Great Lakes

Mississippi

•Toronto

•New York
•Washington

ATLANTIC OCEAN

•Mexico City

Caribbean Sea

Equator

Amazon

SOUTH AMERICA

Rio de Janeiro•

Santiago •

•Buenos Aires

KEY

ICE

TUNDRA

CONIFEROUS FOREST

TEMPERATE FOREST

TROPICAL FOREST

GRASSLAND

DESERT

MOUNTAINS

12

These two foxes – the arctic fox (right) and the kit fox (left) – are made for very different climates. The arctic fox's short ears lose little body heat. This helps to keep it warm in the cold lands of the far north. The kit fox has large ears, which lose body heat. This helps it to keep cool in North America's hot deserts.

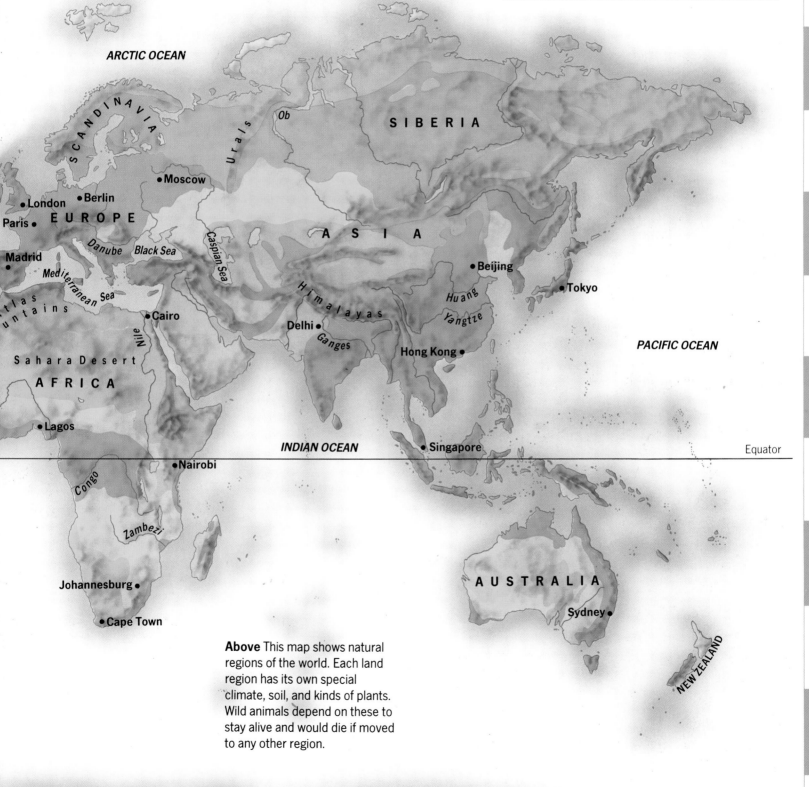

ARCTIC

ARCTIC OCEAN

SCANDINAVIA

Urals

Ob

SIBERIA

• Moscow

• London • Berlin

EUROPE

Paris •

Danube   Black Sea

Caspian Sea

ASIA

Madrid •

Mediterranean Sea

• Beijing

• Tokyo

Atlas Mountains

Himalayas

Huang

• Cairo

Nile

Delhi •

Yangtze

Sahara Desert

Ganges

Hong Kong •

PACIFIC OCEAN

AFRICA

• Lagos

INDIAN OCEAN   • Singapore

Equator

• Nairobi

Congo

Zambezi

AUSTRALIA

Johannesburg •

Sydney •

• Cape Town

Above This map shows natural regions of the world. Each land region has its own special climate, soil, and kinds of plants. Wild animals depend on these to stay alive and would die if moved to any other region.

NEW ZEALAND

ANTARCTIC

COLD LANDS

The far north and far south are among the coldest places on Earth. Summers there are short and cool, but winters are long, dark, and freezing.

In the Arctic, the far north, lies land called tundra. There, mosses, flowers, and tiny trees manage to grow. They can be seen when the snow melts at the end of the long winter. The frozen ground below the surface never melts, even in the middle of summer.

Tundra animals survive winters cold enough to kill most creatures. Musk-oxen can stand temperatures as low as −158 degrees Fahrenheit (−70 degrees Celsius). They have dense, fleecy coats to keep out the cold. Caribou have coats of specially adapted hairs that keep them warm. Both kinds of animals find their food in winter by pawing away the snow and nibbling the plants beneath.

Their main enemies are wolves. Packs of wolves chase herds of caribou and musk-oxen and kill old, weak, or injured animals.

In winter, some creatures, such as arctic hares, grow white coats, the color of the snow, to help them hide from predators. This blending with their surroundings is called camouflage. Their predators – arctic foxes, stoats, polar bears, and snowy owls – also have white coats as camouflage.

Above A harp seal suckles its pup on sea ice off eastern Canada. A layer of thick fat called blubber protects seals' bodies from cold seawater.

Below Polar bears roam the edges of the land and swim out to ice to hunt for seals. Dense, waterproof fur keeps these bears warm.

Arctic camouflage

In summer, the ptarmigan's dark plumage (below left) is hard to see on the ground. In winter, the ptarmigan and the willow grouse (below right) turn white to match the snow. Camouflage that changes with the seasons hides these birds from enemies.

Below Northern continents almost cut off the Arctic Ocean from warm ocean currents flowing from the south. Ice covers the middle of this chilly ocean all year round, and much more in the winter.

KEY

☐ ICE

▨ TUNDRA

Above Only low-growing plants survive the freezing winds that sweep across the Arctic in winter. Cold kills the tips of any trees that grow even waist-high.

Extent of ice in winter

Extent of ice in summer

ALASKA

NORTH AMERICA

SIBERIA

ASIA

North Pole

ARCTIC OCEAN

GREENLAND

SCANDINAVIA

EUROPE

Extent of ice in winter

ICELAND

Antarctic land animals

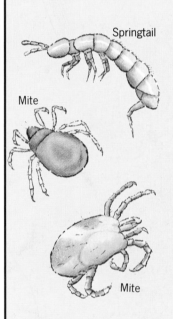

Springtail

Mite

Mite

No backboned animals spend all their time on the icy southern continent of Antarctica. Seals, penguins, and most birds that live there find food at sea. The largest Antarctic animals that live on land all year round are tiny insects and mites. Little jumping insects called springtails live in mosses. Eight-legged mites are relatives of spiders. Antarctic mites live mainly on lichens growing on rocks. Mites and springtails (shown above much larger than life-size) can live close to the South Pole, where temperatures fall as low as −149°F (−65°C).

Right Reindeer can live in colder lands than any other deer. Hollow hairs trap air that helps to insulate their bodies from the cold. So does their undercoat of dense, soft fur. In winter, reindeer paw away the snow to eat the lichens growing on the ground beneath. This is how they earned their Native American name, caribou, meaning "shoveler." Their broad splayed hooves also spread their weight, which helps them walk on snow or boggy ground. These are the only deer whose females as well as males grow antlers. A female will use these to drive other deer from the winter feeding ground she keeps clear for herself and her calf.

MOUNTAINS: NORTH AND SOUTH AMERICA

High mountains everywhere are bare, steep, and always very cold and windy. The higher you climb, the colder, thinner, and windier the air becomes. Even at the equator (usually the warmest part of the world, around the middle), thick snow and ice lie on high mountain peaks. Yet, somehow, mountain animals survive. Their bodies are adapted to life there – mammals have thick fur to keep them warm and some can climb the steepest slopes.

In the Rocky Mountains of North America, bighorn sheep and Rocky Mountain goats leap from rock to rock among the crags. This is how they stay safe from their enemies, the big cats known as pumas. Smaller animals such as squirrels and pikas are in greater danger – eagles may swoop down and seize them.

Guanacos and vicuñas graze on the grassy slopes of South America's Andes mountains. These long-legged relatives of camels can run fast to escape danger. Smaller animals, such as the little rodents called chinchillas and viscachas, dig burrows to hide from their enemies, and a whole flock of finches will huddle under rocks for warmth.

Some Andean birds hide their nests in burrows. Using only its beak and claws, a small bird called a ground tyrant digs a nest burrow three feet (one meter) long.

Above A condor soars high above the Andes. This giant vulture scans the mountains in search of dead animals to eat.

Below A puma (or "mountain lion" or "cougar"). These hunters roam the mountains of western North and South America.

Life zones

Different plants and animals live at different levels on mountain slopes. This diagram shows North America's Sierra Nevada mountain range. Eagles soar among the high peaks, more than 12,000 ft (3,600 m) above sea level. Lower down, lynxes hunt their prey among pine forests. In the lower, open countryside there are jackrabbits. Lizards and other desert dwellers survive on the driest slopes.

Eagle

Lynx

Jackrabbit

Lizard

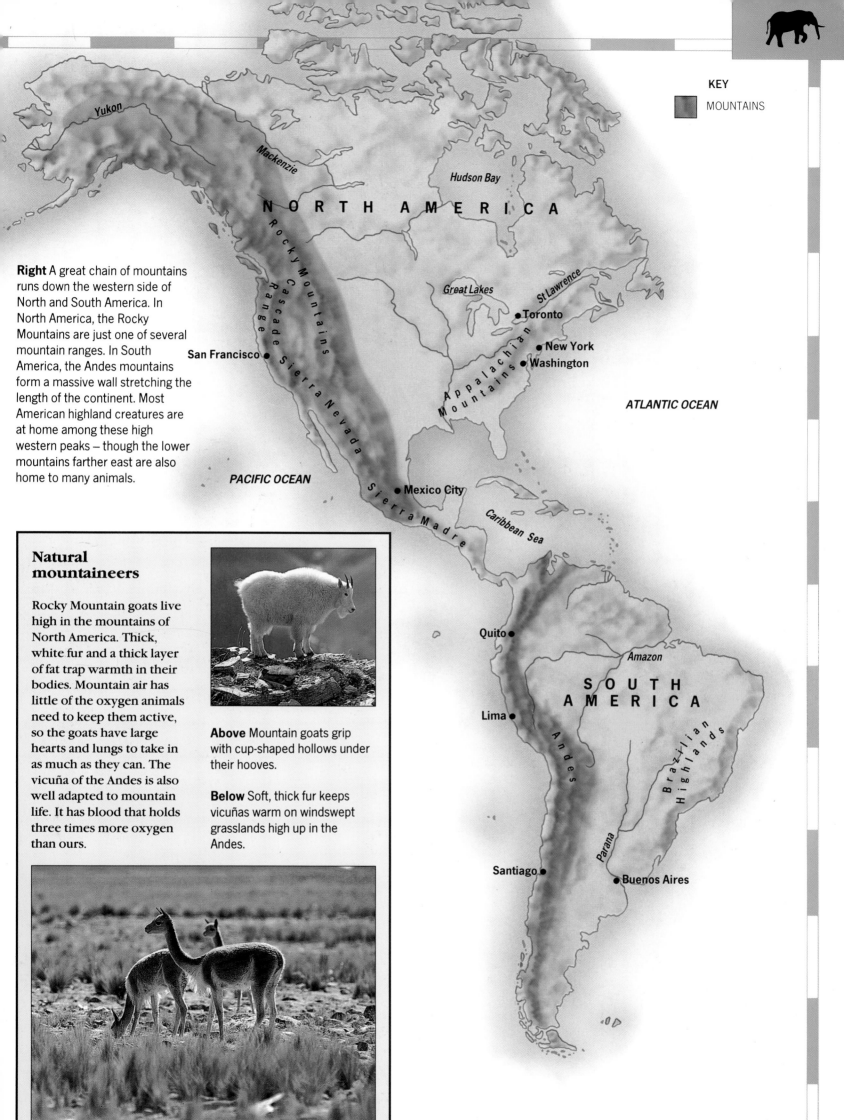

Right A great chain of mountains runs down the western side of North and South America. In North America, the Rocky Mountains are just one of several mountain ranges. In South America, the Andes mountains form a massive wall stretching the length of the continent. Most American highland creatures are at home among these high western peaks – though the lower mountains farther east are also home to many animals.

Yukon

Mackenzie

Hudson Bay

NORTH AMERICA

Rocky Mountains

Cascade Range

Sierra Nevada

Great Lakes

St Lawrence

● Toronto

● New York

● Washington

Appalachian Mountains

ATLANTIC OCEAN

San Francisco ●

PACIFIC OCEAN

● Mexico City

Sierra Madre

Caribbean Sea

Quito ●

Amazon

SOUTH AMERICA

Lima ●

Andes

Brazilian Highlands

Parana

Santiago ●

● Buenos Aires

Natural mountaineers

Rocky Mountain goats live high in the mountains of North America. Thick, white fur and a thick layer of fat trap warmth in their bodies. Mountain air has little of the oxygen animals need to keep them active, so the goats have large hearts and lungs to take in as much as they can. The vicuña of the Andes is also well adapted to mountain life. It has blood that holds three times more oxygen than ours.

Above Mountain goats grip with cup-shaped hollows under their hooves.

Below Soft, thick fur keeps vicuñas warm on windswept grasslands high up in the Andes.

MOUNTAINS: EUROPE AND ASIA

A long chain of mountains runs from Spain and northwestern Africa through Europe and Asia. The spiky Alps and Asia's Himalayas, the highest peaks on Earth, rise here. These mountains are home to hardy and surefooted animals.

The largest mountain animals are yaks, which are found in Tibet. Yaks are cattle with long, thick hair. This keeps them warm when it is so cold that most other animals would die.

The nimblest mountaineers are mountain goats and sheep and the goatlike chamois. A chamois can jump thirty feet (nine meters) and land safely.

Rodents live on more level ground. Alpine voles and alpine marmots both spend winter underground. Alpine marmots spend nearly half the year in a kind of deep sleep called hibernation.

These small rodents must watch out for foxes, stoats, and eagles. Even larger hunters roam high Asian mountains. Here, snow leopards hunt yak calves and ibexes. There are also little mountain hunters such as wallcreepers — birds that pluck insects from the crevices in cliffs.

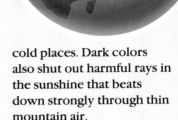

Mountain butterflies

The Apollo butterfly lives in the Himalayas. Its dull color helps it to survive in the harsh climate of the mountains. Small mountain creatures of all kinds – from butterflies to salamanders – are often drably colored. Creatures with dark skins or wings warm up quickly in the sun. This is important in cold places. Dark colors also shut out harmful rays in the sunshine that beats down strongly through thin mountain air.

Mountain heights

This diagram shows some of the mountains in Europe and Asia and compares their heights. (Mount Kilimanjaro is also included as it is the tallest peak in Africa.) The peaks of high mountains are usually covered with snow. Lower down the slopes, where it is usually a bit warmer, there is enough plant life to support animals. Mountains in the far north do not have to be very high before their peaks are permanently covered with snow, even during the summer months.

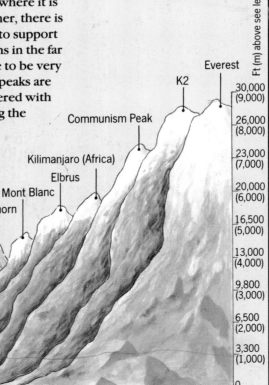

Vesuvius
Ben Nevis
Sinai
Olympus
Etna
Mulhacen
Fujiyama
Matterhorn
Mont Blanc
Elbrus
Kilimanjaro (Africa)
Communism Peak
K2
Everest

Ft (m) above sea level

30,000 (9,000)
26,000 (8,000)
23,000 (7,000)
20,000 (6,000)
16,500 (5,000)
13,000 (4,000)
9,800 (3,000)
6,500 (2,000)
3,300 (1,000)
0

Above Lammergeiers are mountain vultures that live as far apart as the Pyrenees and the Himalayas. They drop the bones of the creatures they eat onto the rocks to get at the marrow inside.

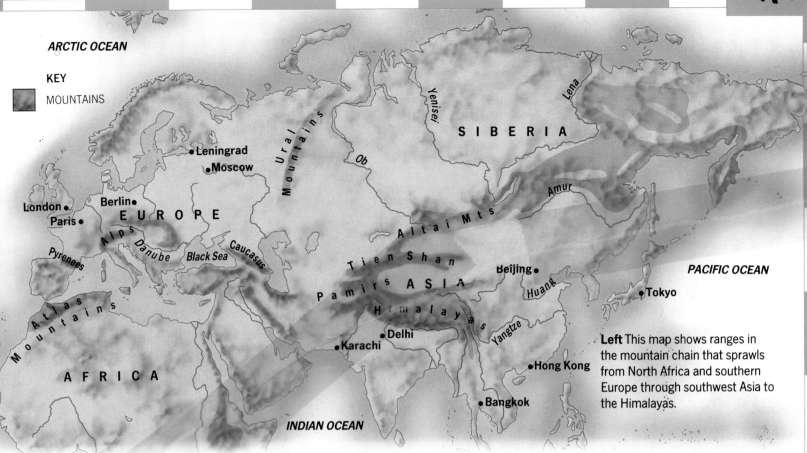

ARCTIC OCEAN

KEY

MOUNTAINS

Leningrad
Moscow
Berlin
London
Paris
EUROPE
Pyrenees
Alps
Danube
Black Sea
Caucasus
Atlas Mountains
AFRICA

Ural Mountains
Ob
Yenisei
Lena
SIBERIA
Amur
Altai Mts
Tien Shan
Pamirs
Himalayas
ASIA
Beijing
Huang
Delhi
Karachi
Yangtze
Hong Kong
Bangkok
Tokyo

PACIFIC OCEAN

INDIAN OCEAN

Left This map shows ranges in the mountain chain that sprawls from North Africa and southern Europe through southwest Asia to the Himalayas.

Islands in the sky

Some animals live only on a few high mountains. They find the plains below too hot or dry or full of enemies, so they cannot spread out from their mountain homes. These creatures are as isolated as if they lived on islands surrounded by sea. Among these stranded animals are a kind of mountain goat from Africa. The Nubian ibex is found only in the highlands of a single nation, Ethiopia.

Above Mount Haramukh's bare slopes are reflected in the chilly waters of a lake at the northern edge of India. On high Himalayan mountainsides, the strong, cold winds and barren rock make life difficult for all but tiny animals, such as spiders.

Right Agile chamois roam craggy slopes of the Gran Paradiso National Park in the Italian Alps. These animals can make great leaps and still land safely – they have 'shock-absorbing' legs and feet. Most troops are led by an old, experienced female. Chamois belong to an unusual group of mammals, sometimes called goat-antelopes.

CONIFEROUS FORESTS: NORTH AMERICA

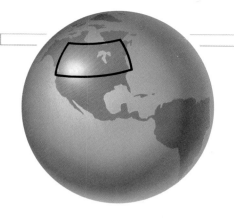

South of the treeless far north a great belt of forest rings the world. This northern forest covers much of Canada and the mountainous areas of the United States. Plants and animals here must make the most of summer, for winter is long and cold.

Most of the trees in this forest are conifers — trees with evergreen, needle-shaped leaves and seeds protected by a woody cone. These trees contain a kind of natural antifreeze that stops their sap from freezing. They have springy branches that bend but do not break beneath the weight of the snow. There are also a few broad-leaved trees that shed their leaves in winter.

These northern forests hold fewer kinds of creatures than forests farther south. Most plant eaters dislike the taste of the sticky resin that conifers produce to guard them from decay. There are few other plants to eat on the bare forest floor. Chipmunks, squirrels, and birds called crossbills eat the seeds inside the woody cones, and porcupines munch bark in winter. Moose eat willows. Wolves hunt deer. Small ground animals fear lynxes, wolverines, and stoats. Even tree climbers are not safe from nimble, climbing martens, or from owls and goshawks swooping from above.

Above A moose, the world's largest deer, browses in boggy clearings in the northern forests.

Below Beavers chew with four long, curved, chisel-like front teeth that keep on growing and never wear out.

Beavers' lodge

Beavers are amazing engineers. Most other rodents just dig a burrow, but many beavers make lakes and island homes.

First, beavers heap mud and stones across a stream bed. Next they use their strong front teeth to cut down trees and gnaw off the branches. Then they push, drag, or roll the logs and branches into the stream and pile them on the heaped-up mud and stones.

Lastly, they plaster mud on the logs and branches to form a dam that blocks the stream, making a lake. In this, the family may build an island home, also made of branches, logs, and mud. Underwater entrances lead inside.

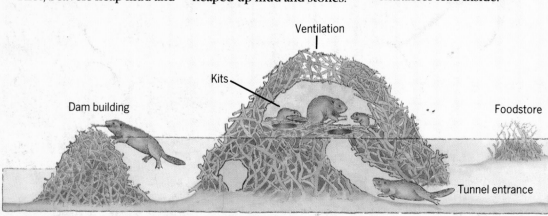

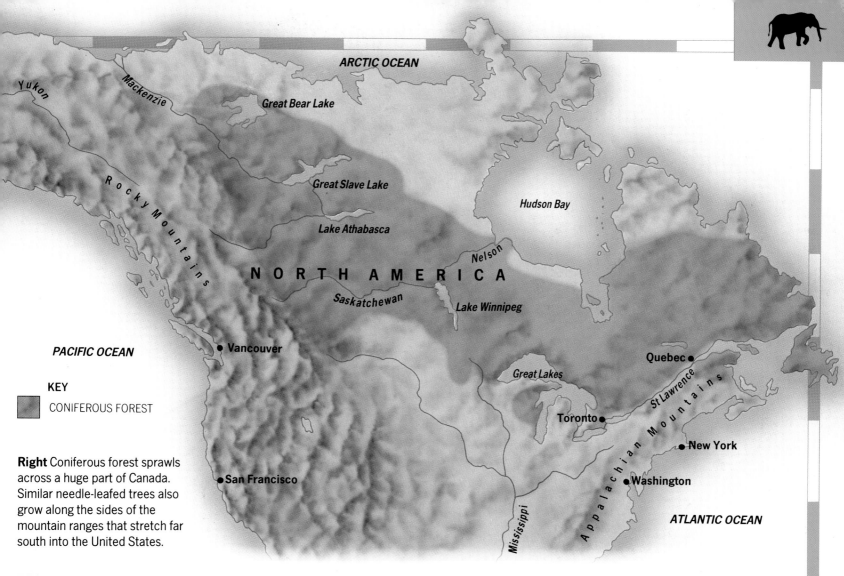

ARCTIC OCEAN

Great Bear Lake

Yukon

Mackenzie

Rocky Mountains

Great Slave Lake

Lake Athabasca

Hudson Bay

NORTH AMERICA

Nelson

Saskatchewan

Lake Winnipeg

PACIFIC OCEAN

Vancouver

Great Lakes

Quebec

KEY

CONIFEROUS FOREST

Toronto

St Lawrence

Appalachian Mountains

New York

San Francisco

Washington

Mississippi

ATLANTIC OCEAN

Right Coniferous forest sprawls across a huge part of Canada. Similar needle-leafed trees also grow along the sides of the mountain ranges that stretch far south into the United States.

Left Hornlike tufts of feathers earn the great horned owl its name. This night hunter has staring yellow eyes and a frightening shriek. The owl kills hares and rabbits, and birds as large as grouse.

Below A northern lynx. Lynxes are hunters, often killing hares. Every few years, the forest hares multiply. There is plenty of food for the lynxes, and so their numbers also increase. Then, mysteriously, the hares start to die. Perhaps they are short of food. When the hares die, many lynxes also starve.

Bears

Black bears are not always black. Some are rusty brown or creamy. Black bears are about 5 ft (1.5 m) long and weigh up to 500 lbs (230 kg), much less than the North American brown bears. Both kinds of bears eat berries, eggs, honey, and nuts but also hunt small mammals such as mice and squirrels. All bears have a flat-footed lumbering walk, but a black bear chasing its prey can run at up to 25 mi (40 km) an hour and even climb a tree. Many thousand black bears roam Canadian and American forests.

People who try feeding the bears can be badly hurt. The bears have uncertain tempers and sharp claws and teeth.

CONIFEROUS FORESTS: EUROPE AND ASIA

Evergreen coniferous forest stretches across northern Europe and Asia from Scandinavia to the Pacific Ocean.

Many of the forest animals that live there have close relatives in North America. Both places have lynxes, brown bears (called grizzly bears in North America), elk (moose), and reindeer (caribou). In both places young mammals are born in spring and grow fast in summer when there is plenty of food.

None of the mammals of the northern European and Asian forests hibernate in winter. Instead, voles and lemmings (both small rodents) tunnel under snow in search of moss or bark to eat. Plump birds called hazel grouse and capercaillie eat seeds on the ground. High above, red squirrels gnaw bark and pinecones, and flying squirrels parachute from tree to tree.

Birds called waxwings eat berries, while crossbills, nutcrackers, and Siberian jays use their powerful beaks for cracking cones open. In summer, rubythroats and other insect-eating birds feast on swarms of hatching insects.

Those low, sleek predators, the pine marten and sable, prowl these forests, along with the much larger hunters, the wolf and wolverine. Large hunting birds of these forests include the eagle owl and great gray owl.

Above Most northern forest trees are conifers. But here and there stand broad-leaved trees. Their dying leaves in the fall are bright against the green.

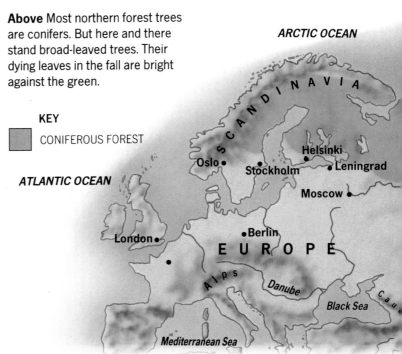

KEY

CONIFEROUS FOREST

ARCTIC OCEAN

SCANDINAVIA

Oslo • • Helsinki
Stockholm • • Leningrad

• Moscow

ATLANTIC OCEAN

London •
• Berlin

EUROPE

Alps
Danube
Black Sea
Cau

Mediterranean Sea

Tree homes

Young owls peer from their nest hole in a tree. In the immense northern forests of Europe and Asia stand countless trees killed off by lightning or disease. Before they finally fall, their decaying tree trunks provide valuable homes for birds that nest in holes. Owls find their homes ready-made, but woodpeckers, working with their pointed beaks, punch out their own nest holes in the softened, rotting timber.

Insects in the conifers

Conifer forests teem with insects. Pine weevils munch tender shoots, while other beetles eat wood or bark. Wood wasps inject eggs into wood through a long, egg-laying tube, and their young eat their way out. Their main enemies are ichneumon wasps. These drill through wood with long, egg-laying tubes and lay eggs on wood wasps still inside a tree. When the ichneumons hatch, they eat the wood wasps.

Above The pine-hawkmoth often rests on pine bark – and its colors match this. Its caterpillars eat pine leaves.

Above Red squirrels are nimble climbers. They eat a range of foods: pinecones and other tree seeds and berries, mushrooms, and even eggs and young birds.

SIBERIA

Lena

Yenisei

Mountains

Ob

Altai Mts

Tien Shan

ASIA

Lake Baikal

Amur

PACIFIC OCEAN

Left From Scandinavia in the west to the Asian Pacific coast in the Far East lies an almost unbroken sea of needle-leaved trees. This is the taiga – the largest forest anywhere.

Left Brown bears are the largest, fiercest carnivores that roam the northern forests of Europe and Asia. Brown bears eat much the same foods as the black bears of North America.

Below Pine martens are small, agile hunters, leaping from tree to tree and running down head first to catch small birds and mammals. They nest in tree holes, birds' nests, and squirrels' nests.

TEMPERATE FORESTS: NORTH AMERICA

The temperate areas of the world are those that lie between the cold places around the poles and the hot tropics around the equator.

Forests of broad-leaved trees once covered much of the temperate parts of North America, Europe, and eastern Asia, south of the great northern forests. Most of these forests have been cut down now.

The trees that grow in what remains of these forests are oaks or hickories and other trees that shed their leaves in winter. As the leaves rot, they become food for plants and shrubs as well as creatures such as worms and beetles. In turn, many of these tiny creatures are eaten by small predators such as shrews, salamanders, and warblers.

Parts of eastern North America are covered with deciduous (leaf-shedding) woodlands like these. White-tailed deer and smaller plant eaters, such as eastern chipmunks, gray squirrels, and white-footed mice, live there. Wild turkeys once strutted everywhere, but few are left now that their habitat has been destroyed and so many have been killed.

Opossums as big as cats hang from trees by their long, bare tails. Black bears prowl the woodland floor. Both eat small animals and plants. The main hunters in these woods are bobcats, foxes, skunks, raccoons, weasels, hawks, and owls. Humans have killed off almost all the wolves and pumas (once the woodlands' largest predators).

Squirrels

Squirrels are tree acrobats, using their sharp claws just as human climbers use spiked climbing boots. Digging its claws into the bark, a squirrel bounds up a tree. Then it runs along a branch on all fours, sometimes upside down. Gray squirrels can even hang from one branch by their hind feet. Many squirrels can leap nearly 14 ft (4 m) between trees, and flying squirrels can make much greater leaps than that as they glide between the trees.

Above The gray squirrel's true home is the American forests.

Below This flying squirrel parachutes on a web of skin between front and hind limbs.

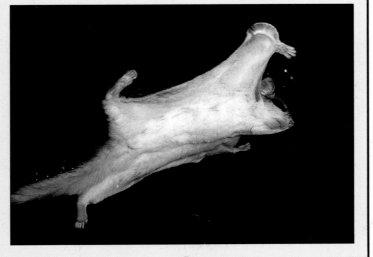

Above North American woodlands are famous for their fall colors. This woodland is in the Appalachian Mountains.

Below The skunk's bold black-and-white pattern is a warning to stay away or you may be sprayed with a horrible-smelling fluid from scent glands beneath its tail.

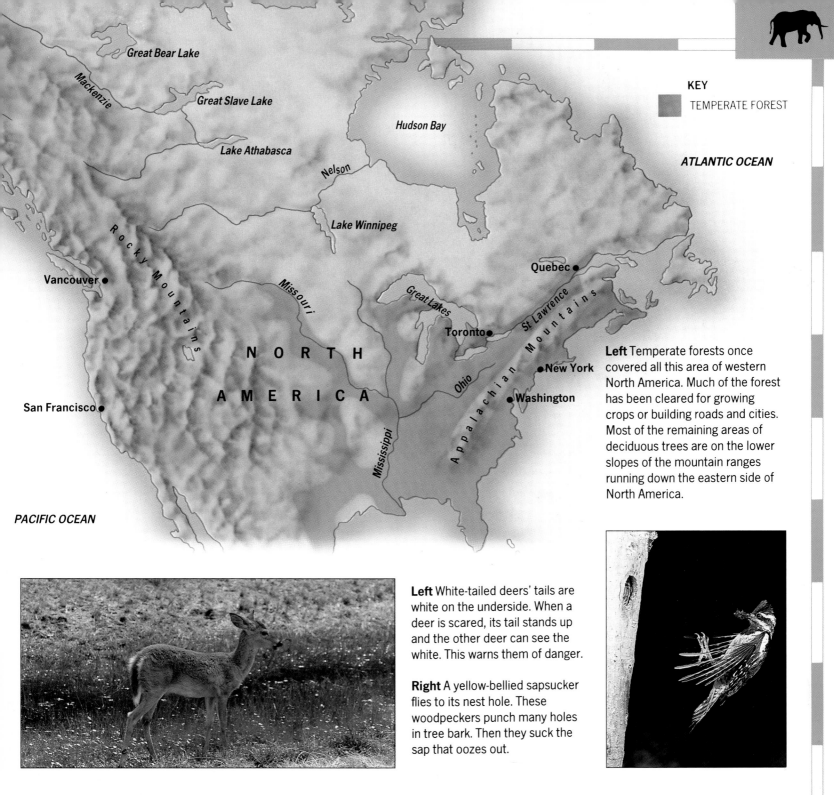

Great Bear Lake

Mackenzie

Great Slave Lake

Lake Athabasca

Hudson Bay

Nelson

Lake Winnipeg

Rocky Mountains

Vancouver ●

Missouri

Great Lakes

Quebec ●

St Lawrence

Appalachian Mountains

Toronto ●

N O R T H

A M E R I C A

Ohio

● New York

San Francisco ●

Mississippi

● Washington

PACIFIC OCEAN

Left Temperate forests once covered all this area of western North America. Much of the forest has been cleared for growing crops or building roads and cities. Most of the remaining areas of deciduous trees are on the lower slopes of the mountain ranges running down the eastern side of North America.

Left White-tailed deers' tails are white on the underside. When a deer is scared, its tail stands up and the other deer can see the white. This warns them of danger.

Right A yellow-bellied sapsucker flies to its nest hole. These woodpeckers punch many holes in tree bark. Then they suck the sap that oozes out.

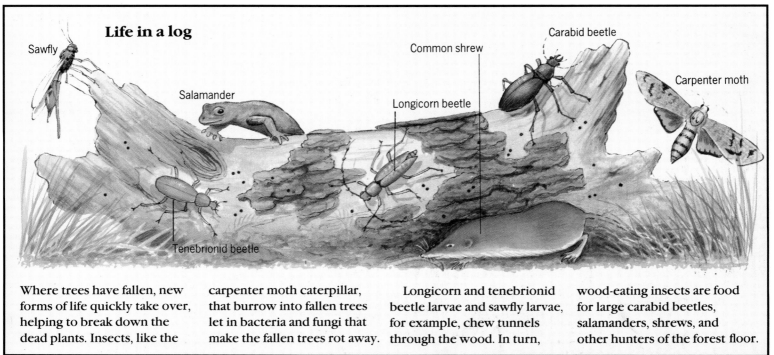

Life in a log

Sawfly

Salamander

Common shrew

Carabid beetle

Longicorn beetle

Carpenter moth

Tenebrionid beetle

Where trees have fallen, new forms of life quickly take over, helping to break down the dead plants. Insects, like the carpenter moth caterpillar, that burrow into fallen trees let in bacteria and fungi that make the fallen trees rot away. Longicorn and tenebrionid beetle larvae and sawfly larvae, for example, chew tunnels through the wood. In turn, wood-eating insects are food for large carabid beetles, salamanders, shrews, and other hunters of the forest floor.

TEMPERATE FORESTS: EUROPE AND ASIA

Deciduous woods and forests are dotted across Europe and parts of eastern Asia. Chestnuts, oaks, beeches, and other broad-leaved trees tower above much smaller shrubs. Flowers, ferns, and mosses grow among dead leaves on the forest floor.

In a forest, there are animals at every level. Rabbits raise young in burrows. Moles tunnel underground, hunting for worms. Shrews, voles, and mice scamper under the fallen leaves.

On the ground, deer and rabbits graze in open glades. In some forests wild boar sniff, nose down, in search of tasty roots and fungi.

Dormice and long-tailed field mice climb among the shrubs eating nuts and seeds. There are red or gray squirrels in the trees. Spotted woodpeckers drill nest holes in tree trunks. Chickadees and warblers perch on twigs to catch insects.

Farther south, where summers are hot and dry, low trees and shrubs grow around the Mediterranean Sea. Most are evergreen with tough or shiny leaves that can endure the scorching summer sunshine. This kind of warm temperate woodland is home to lizards, snakes, rabbits, and birds such as nightingales.

KEY

TEMPERATE FOREST

ARCTIC OCEAN

Leningrad
Moscow
Berlin
London
Paris
EUROPE
Rhine
Volga
ATLANTIC OCEAN
Alps
Danube
Caspian
Rome
Black Sea
Madrid
Ankara
Algiers
Tigris
Euphrates
Mediterranean Sea

Hibernation

As winter starts, a dormouse falls asleep. It grows almost as cold as the air around its nest. Its breathing and heartbeat become so slow that it can seem quite dead. In the coldest weather, its body warms up just enough to keep it from freezing. In long winters, dormice hibernate for more than half the year. Hibernating dormice can last months without eating because they need so little energy. They get the little they need from the food they ate before they fell asleep. In the fall, dormice grow plump by eating extra nuts and

Above A dormouse gathering fall berries.

berries. They turn this food into body fat, which helps to nourish them until they feed again next spring.

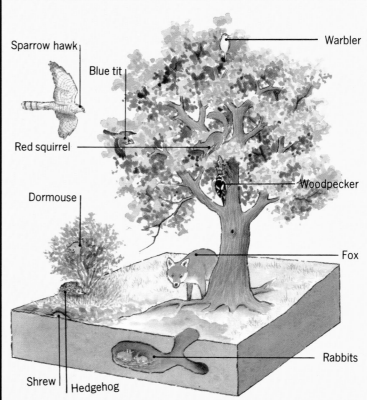

Sparrow hawk
Blue tit
Warbler
Red squirrel
Dormouse
Woodpecker
Fox
Rabbits
Shrew | Hedgehog

Levels of life

This European woodland provides homes for a variety of creatures. A warbler sings high in an oak tree, a red squirrel climbs among its branches, and a greater spotted woodpecker drills a nest in decaying wood. Meanwhile a sparrow hawk swoops down on a blue tit. Lower down, a dormouse rests in a shrub, a hedgehog hunts for beetles, and a shrew looks for earthworms. A red fox watches out for rabbits.

Ob
Yenisei
Lena
Lake Baikal
Amur

ASIA

Himalayas

Huang
• Beijing
Vladivostok

Yangtze

PACIFIC OCEAN

• Tokyo

• Delhi
• Karachi

Hong Kong •

INDIAN
OCEAN

Above Trees shut out light from the forest floor, and few plants can grow beneath these beeches. In woodlands flowers bloom in the spring, before the leaves block out the light.

Left Temperate forests once covered most of western Europe and Asia. Now only patches of forest are left.

Left In summer, purple emperor butterflies fly among the trees. Like other butterflies, they sip nectar, but they also feed on dead rabbits and other animals lying on the ground. Their caterpillars eat willow leaves.

Above The sparrow hawk is a fast, agile flier, dashing between the trees. It swoops down on unsuspecting small birds, such as blue tits.

Below In spring, jays steal and eat the eggs and young of other birds. In the fall they bury acorns and dig them up again in winter when other kinds of food are scarce.

Night hunters

As dusk falls, foxes and badgers leave their holes and prowl in search of food. Keen senses help them. Foxes hunt rabbits, mice, and birds, but they will also eat earthworms, berries, buds, and seeds. They sometimes dig out wild bees' nests to steal the honey. Like foxes, badgers will snap up anything they can, including worms, snails, insects, eggs, acorns, berries, roots, and mushrooms.

PRAIRIE LIFE

A broad sea of grasses once covered the middle of North America from the Gulf of Mexico north through the United States into Canada. This was the prairie. Now, little of the grassland remains, and most of the area is used as farmland to grow crops or as cattle ranches.

Plant-eating prairie animals eat the roots, stems, leaves, or seeds of grasses or other soft-stemmed plants. Low plants or the soil beneath hide many of the smaller creatures from their enemies and from the freezing winter winds.

Those large prairie animals the bison (a type of wild cattle) and the antelope-like pronghorns escape from their enemies by running fast. They have dense coats that protect their bodies from the winter cold.

In spring, the prairie echoes with strange booming sounds. The noisemakers are male prairie grouse showing off to win mates. Prairie grouse and the little ground squirrels called prairie dogs are the favorite foods of predators that prowl these open lands. Badgers, foxes, pumas, hawks, coyotes, and eagles are always on the lookout for a meal.

Prairie dogs

Prairie dogs are not dogs, but burrowing ground squirrels. They live in large groups, in a mass of burrows. Groups of burrows can form very large underground "towns" each with 500 prairie dogs or more. Burrowing owls and snakes may also live there, as unwelcome guests. Some prairie dogs keep a lookout and bark, like dogs, as a warning when they see an enemy. When they hear the bark, nearby prairie dogs dive down their burrows for safety.

Below Coyotes are doglike hunter-scavengers. They kill rabbits and small rodents and eat any dead animal they find.

Many-chambered stomachs

Many grassland animals, such as cattle and deer, are "ruminants" – animals with a special kind of digestive system. The grass they swallow first goes to a chamber called the rumen, where tiny organisms break it down. It then returns to the mouth for more chewing. Then it passes through two stomach chambers before reaching the abomasum, where proteins are broken down. This ensures that ruminants extract all the goodness they can from their food. Horses have a different kind of digestive system. The grass goes straight to the stomach where it is digested as much as possible, but some is left to pass out of the body.

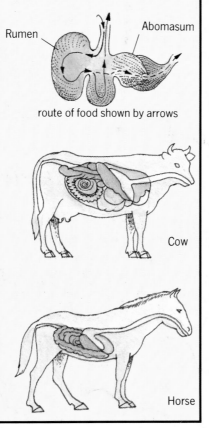

Rumen

Abomasum

route of food shown by arrows

Cow

Horse

Below This map shows the great belt of grassland that once covered much of North America before farms took its place. Small patches of true prairie remain. The grass grows high and thick on the moist eastern prairie. Nearer the Rockies in the west, the land is drier and grasses are shorter and grow farther apart.

Left In spring, male sage grouse strut to show off to a group of females, and two males will often have a fight. The winner will mate with most of the females.

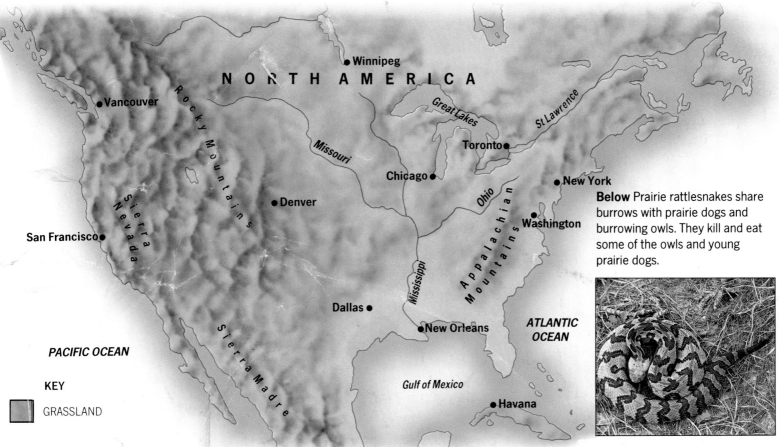

NORTH AMERICA

Winnipeg

Vancouver

Rocky Mountains

Great Lakes

St Lawrence

Missouri

Toronto

Chicago

New York

Denver

Sierra Nevada

Ohio

Washington

San Francisco

Appalachian Mountains

Mississippi

Below Prairie rattlesnakes share burrows with prairie dogs and burrowing owls. They kill and eat some of the owls and young prairie dogs.

Dallas

New Orleans

ATLANTIC OCEAN

PACIFIC OCEAN

Sierra Madre

KEY

GRASSLAND

Gulf of Mexico

Havana

Right Bison are big wild cattle with huge shoulders, shaggy hair, and short curved horns. A big bull bison weighs nearly a ton (1,000 kg). Millions of bison used to roam the prairies before farmers and ranchers drove them out and hunters killed them off. Far smaller numbers now survive and only on protected land. Before fences blocked their path, great bison herds migrated south in the fall to avoid the harshest winter weather. In spring the herds wandered slowly north again and ate the fresh grass sprouting where the snow had thawed.

STEPPE ANIMALS

A band of grassland called the steppe stretches across northern Asia from west to east. Much has been plowed up. What is left looks very much like the North American prairie.

When spring comes, the snow melts and the steppe is bright with irises and other flowers. In summer, feathery grasses ripple in the wind.

Saiga antelopes wander here, as do great bustards – the world's largest flying birds. These are as big as swans and stride around in flocks, pecking at plants and insects and gobbling up voles.

Rodents make burrows. The largest of these animals are the marmots, which are twice the size of a guinea pig. Smaller rodents include hamsters. The strangest rodents are the blind, tailless mole rats – the world's best burrowers. A mole rat digs tunnels more than 1,300 feet (400 meters) long in its search for roots to eat.

A burrowing animal is not completely safe from predators. Steppe polecats and marbled polecats dig them up or chase them while they are underground. Above ground, they must watch the sky for swooping steppe eagles.

Soil mixers

Burrowing animals like the suslik can change the kind of plants that grow in different parts of the steppe. When they burrow, they bring huge loads of soil to the surface. If this subsoil is different from the soil above it, then existing plants will die and new ones may be able to grow. For example, if the susliks bring salty subsoil to the surface, only salt-resistant plants will survive there. But if they bring chalky soil to the surface in an area where the topsoil was previously salty, then grasses can begin to grow.

Above Susliks are a kind of ground squirrel. They hibernate in winter.

Above Demoiselle cranes breed in the steppe and semi-desert lands, even where the steppe has been cultivated and is covered in great fields of wheat. Each pair performs courtship dances, and the female lays eggs in a nest scraped in the ground. These cranes fly south for the winter, to escape the bitter cold. They return in spring.

Right The area known as the "steppe" stretches from central Europe into Asia. Once a huge area of rolling grassland, much of it is now farmed. The wildlife that once lived there is scarcer than in the past – its habitat having disappeared under plowed fields. It is still home for the strange-looking saiga antelope, as well as for a host of small burrowing animals and birds of many kinds.

ARCTIC OCE

Lening

Berlin

Rhine

E U R O P E

Alps

Danube

Black Sea

Mediterranean Sea

Left Steppe eagles hunt susliks and wild bird chicks. They also feed on creatures that they find already dead. Steppe eagles usually nest on the ground but sometimes build in low trees.

Right The common hamster comes out to feed at night. By day it hides in a maze of burrows, some 8 ft (2.5 m) deep. In the fall it fills storage chambers with carrots, maize, or other food. This hamster sleeps for most of the winter but now and then wakes up to take a snack.

Great bustard

This huge bird (right) weighs up to 35 lbs (16 kg) and can fly! In spring, bustards leave their winter homes in the south. Groups gather in their nesting sites on the steppe, and the males display to the females. After mating, each female lays two or three eggs, in a hollow she has scraped in the ground. Soon after hatching chicks leave the nest and can fly by the time they are five weeks old. The young eat insects. Older birds also eat leaves, flowers, and seeds. These foods, and the bustards themselves, are less common on the steppe now, as farms have taken the place of wild grassland.

Right A male great bustard displaying to attract a mate.

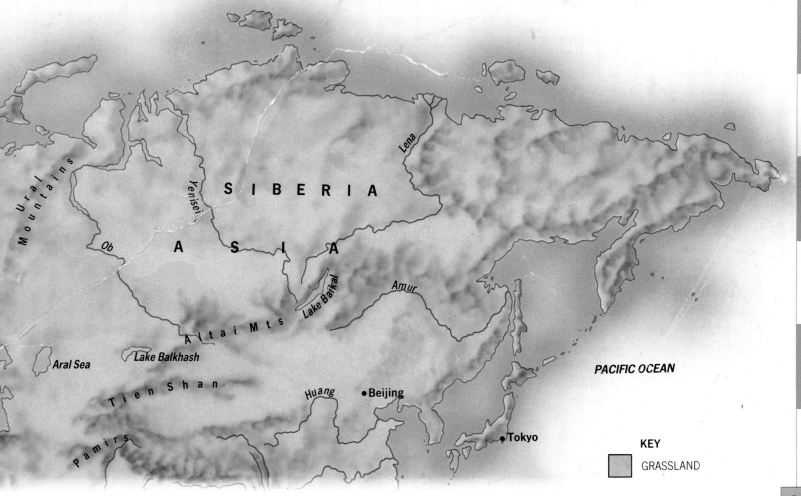

KEY

GRASSLAND

PAMPAS AND LLANOS

Windy grasslands called pampas once covered a chunk of southeastern South America. Farms and ranches now take up most of the land, but the rest still has wild pampas plants and animals. Farther north, there are hot grasslands and, in Patagonia in the south, there are dry, stony steppe grasslands.

Many pampas animals live in the open. The pampas guinea pig nests below a tuft of grass. The chickenlike tinamou lays eggs in a hollow.

The largest mammals are the rare pampas deer and the guanaco. This long-necked relative of the camel lives in mountain pastures, too. Pampas mammals share open plains with rheas, big grayish birds built somewhat like an ostrich.

As on the steppes and prairies, there are many burrowing animals. These include the bushy-tailed viscacha, maras (Patagonian hares), and the small tuco-tucos. These animals get their name from the noise they make inside their holes. All these animals have their enemies, such as the pampas fox and weasel and the long-legged, fast-running maned wolf.

Above Large, flightless birds called rheas have their home on the pampas. They can run as quickly as a horse can gallop.

Life on the *llanos*

The pampas is only one of several areas of South American grassland. In the north of the continent lie the hot grasslands of the *llanos*. This is home to some of the world's strangest animals. Giant anteaters with their long, bushy tails tear open ants' nests with their powerful claws and catch ants on a long, sticky tongue. Armadillos, too, have sticky tongues for catching insects. Bands of bony plates across the back protect an armadillo from its enemies. A scared armadillo rolls up into a ball, as a hedgehog does, or quickly digs itself into the ground. Along *llanos* and forest riversides live capybaras. These are the world's biggest rodents. A capybara can grow as long as a six-year-old child and twice as heavy. Capybaras usually live half-submerged in water, like little hippopotamuses. They graze on shore but plunge into the water if they are afraid of being attacked. They are excellent swimmers and divers.

Right Nine banded armadillos sit near their burrow. Their body armor is not their best defense – their burrows are. They can dig amazingly fast.

Below The giant anteater uses its strong claws to rip open ants' nests. Its sticky tongue, more than 12 in (30 cm) long, licks up the ants.

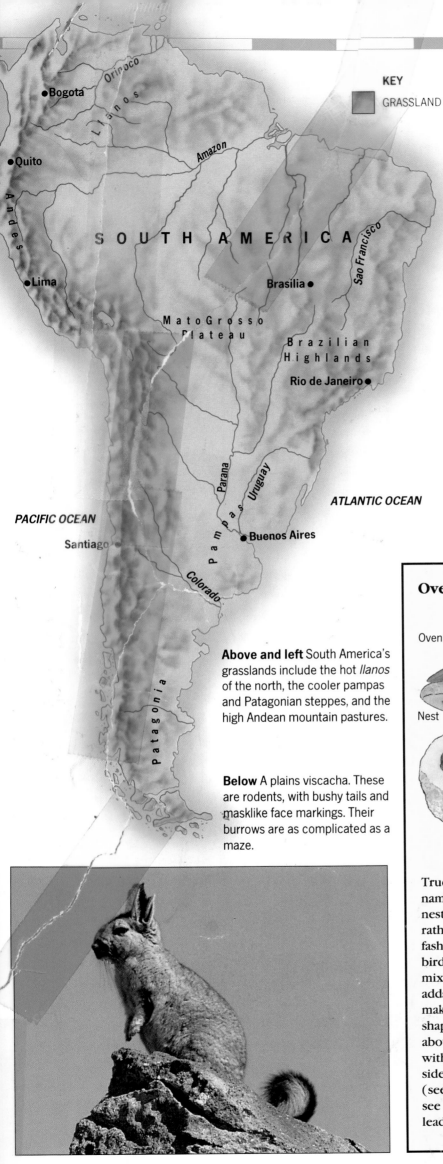

KEY

GRASSLAND

S O U T H   A M E R I C A

Bogota
Quito
Lima
Brasilia
MatoGrosso Plateau
Brazilian Highlands
Rio de Janeiro
Santiago
Buenos Aires
PACIFIC OCEAN
ATLANTIC OCEAN
Patagonia

Above and left South America's grasslands include the hot *llanos* of the north, the cooler pampas and Patagonian steppes, and the high Andean mountain pastures.

Below A plains viscacha. These are rodents, with bushy tails and masklike face markings. Their burrows are as complicated as a maze.

Ovenbirds

Ovenbird

Nest

Entrance   Chamber

True ovenbirds get their name from their mud nests, which are shaped rather like an old-fashioned oven. First the bird makes a cup of clay mixed with grass. Then it adds on to the walls to make them into a dome-shaped roof. It will be about 2 in (4 cm) thick, with an entrance in the side. If it was cut open (see above), you would see a curved passage leading to a nest chamber.

Above Grassland covers large tracts of the Andes, which run down the western side of South America. The pampas and the *llanos* of the lowlands can stretch away, as flat as a table top, as far as you can see.

Below The double-striped thick-knee, or stone, curlew belongs to a group of birds with unusually swollen knee joints. This thick-knee lives on the hot grasslands of northern South America. It runs with short steps across the ground, pausing now and then to stand bolt upright. Thick-knees eat small animals and lay their eggs in a 'saucer' nest, which they scrape out of bare ground.

THE SAVANNAS OF AFRICA

Africa's savannas are huge areas of hot, mostly very dry grassland. For a few months every year there is rain, and the grasses grow as tall as an adult person. Then come dry months when the grass turns dead and yellow. The only trees to survive are those that are well adapted to drought, such as the fat-trunked baobab trees and prickly acacias with umbrella-shaped tops.

Savanna plants help to feed billions of insects from locusts (big grasshoppers) to blind white termites. Spiders, scorpions, and hunting insects called mantids kill and eat many of these creatures. All these creatures are food for bee eaters and other insect-eating birds, while larger birds, such as ground hornbills, eat lizards and small mammals.

African savannas hold more big, wild animals than any other place on Earth. Huge herds of antelopes, wildebeest, and zebras roam the grassy plains, nibbling grasses and leafy shrubs. Giraffes feed on tree leaves too high for other animals to reach. Elephants chew the leaves and bark of trees.

Fierce meat eaters prey upon the herds. A group of lions will ambush a weak wildebeest or zebra. Packs of hyenas and hunting dogs can kill these animals too, by chasing them until they are too tired to run. Jackals and vultures squabble over the hunters' leftovers.

Above Even though they are so tall, giraffes are well camouflaged. The pattern on their skin blends with the shadows of the leaves they eat.

Above Gazelles, grassland, and a flat-topped acacia tree form a scene typical of the East African savanna. Moister savanna has more trees, while drier savanna has hardly any trees at all. All but the driest savanna has enough grass and other plants to feed large numbers of big, wild grazing and browsing mammals.

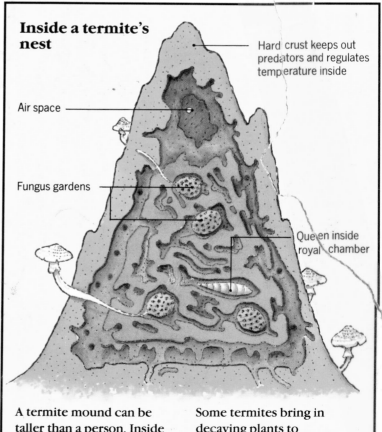

Inside a termite's nest

Hard crust keeps out predators and regulates temperature inside

Air space

Fungus gardens

Queen inside royal chamber

A termite mound can be taller than a person. Inside its hard crust the Queen in her royal chamber lays thousands of eggs each day.

Some termites bring in decaying plants to encourage fungus to grow. They use the fungus for food.

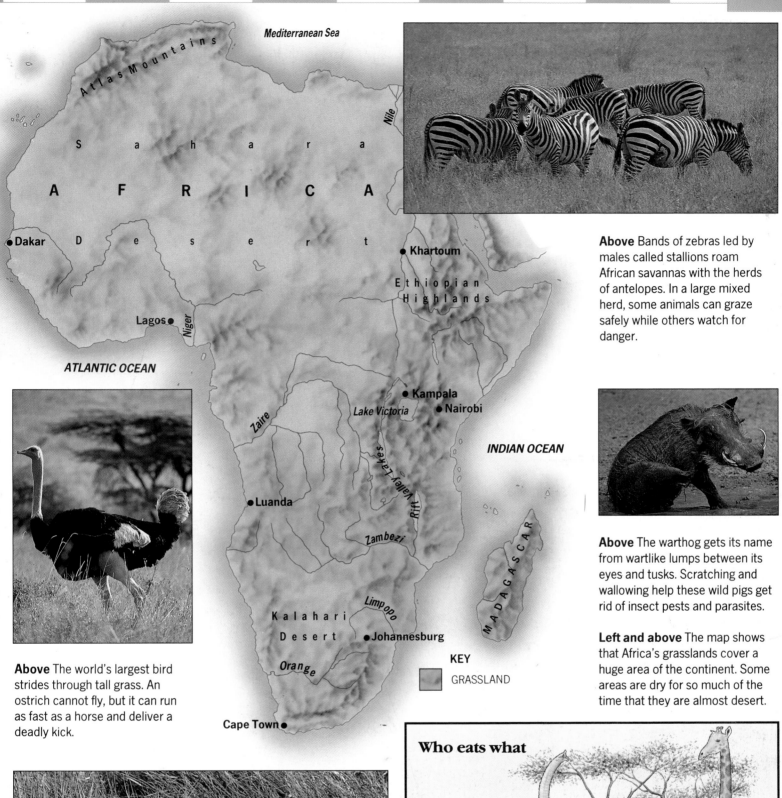

Mediterranean Sea

Atlas Mountains

S a h a r a

A F R I C A

Nile

• Dakar

D e s e r t

• Khartoum

Ethiopian Highlands

Niger

Lagos•

ATLANTIC OCEAN

Zaire

• Kampala

Lake Victoria

• Nairobi

INDIAN OCEAN

• Luanda

Rift Valley Lakes

Zambezi

M A D A G A S C A R

Limpopo

K a l a h a r i
D e s e r t

• Johannesburg

Orange

KEY

GRASSLAND

Cape Town •

Above Bands of zebras led by males called stallions roam African savannas with the herds of antelopes. In a large mixed herd, some animals can graze safely while others watch for danger.

Above The world's largest bird strides through tall grass. An ostrich cannot fly, but it can run as fast as a horse and deliver a deadly kick.

Above The warthog gets its name from wartlike lumps between its eyes and tusks. Scratching and wallowing help these wild pigs get rid of insect pests and parasites.

Left and above The map shows that Africa's grasslands cover a huge area of the continent. Some areas are dry for so much of the time that they are almost desert.

Above Lion cubs enjoy a meal of wildebeest in an African game reserve. A big meat meal will last an adult lion for days. A well-fed pride, or group, of lions spends much time just lying down, digesting food and dozing in the shade. Passing wildebeest are safe until the lions feel hungry and begin to hunt again.

Who eats what

Elephant

Giraffe

Eland

Warthog

Steenbok   White rhinoceros

Plant eaters sharing the same areas of savanna eat different things. This means lots of different animals can all find enough to eat even though they live and feed in the same place. They do not compete with each other.

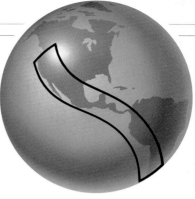

Left Saguaro cactuses soar like organ pipes above the desert floor. It does not rain here very often. When it does, the cactus roots can quickly suck up moisture to store in their fat stems. Sharp spines on the stems protect them from thirsty animals.

DESERTS OF AMERICA

Deserts are the driest places in the world.

In southwestern North America bare rock and sand cover much of the Great Basin and nearby deserts. Mountain ranges shut them off from the moist winds that bring rain from the Pacific Ocean. Sometimes showers do fall, but in summer, moisture soon dries out in the sun.

Only specially adapted plants and animals can survive the desert drought and blazing heat. Cactuses suck up rainwater and store it in their fat stems. After rain, seeds of fast-growing plants sprout and soon produce new plants. These make seeds of their own before they dry up and die.

Cactuses and seeds provide many plant eaters with both moisture and food. Little jumping kangaroo rats get both these from the seeds they eat. Pack rats feed on juicy cactuses. Hunters, such as kit foxes, elf owls, lizards, snakes, and scorpions all survive by eating plant eaters.

Besides getting food and moisture, desert animals must shelter from their enemies and the fierce summer sun. Bony armor guards tortoises against attack, but even they burrow to escape the midday heat.

By day the desert seems empty and lifeless. But as the sun sinks and the air cools, it is alive with little creatures that have spent the hottest hours hidden underground.

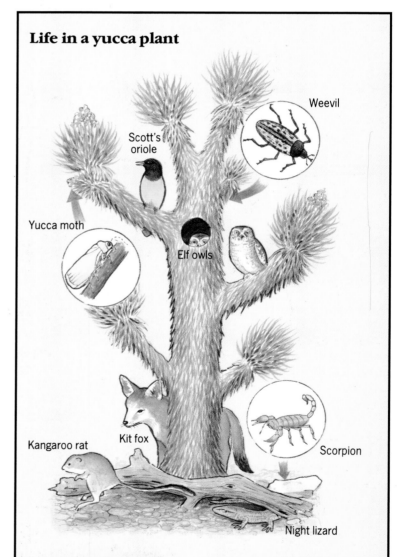

Life in a yucca plant

Weevil

Scott's oriole

Yucca moth

Elf owls

Kangaroo rat

Kit fox

Scorpion

Night lizard

Yucca trees, like this one, and the tall saguaro cactus plants act as 'apartments' for desert animals. Scott's orioles build nests among a yucca's spiny leaves. Gila woodpeckers peck out nest holes, which may be used later by owls or hawks. Yucca weevils feed on the plant itself, while yucca moth grubs eat yucca seeds. Fallen yucca leaves and stems provide homes or food for ground-dwelling insects and other small creatures. Larger animals such as the kit fox come, in turn, to prey on them.

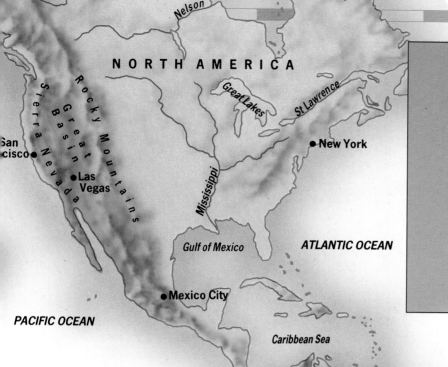

NORTH AMERICA

Nelson

Rocky Mountains

Great Basin

Sierra Nevada

San cisco

Las Vegas

Great Lakes

St Lawrence

Mississippi

New York

Gulf of Mexico

ATLANTIC OCEAN

PACIFIC OCEAN

Mexico City

Caribbean Sea

Right North America's deserts lie east of mountains near the Pacific Ocean. Moist sea winds shed rain on the mountains, leaving none to fall inland. South America's deserts lie near the Pacific because a cold ocean current stops rain from falling here.

Quito

Amazon

SOUTH

AMERICA

Lima

Andes

Atacama Desert

Rio de Janeiro

Parana

Santiago

Buenos Aires

Patagonia

KEY

DESERT

Above The desert scorpion is able to survive both bitter cold and burning summer heat. A poisonous sting in its tail is used for killing enemies and prey.

Below Kangaroo rats get their name from the way they bound along on long hind legs, like kangaroos.

Above The curved-billed thrasher lives among the cactuses of the deserts of the southwestern United States. It builds its nest in a tangle of cactus spines.

Below This desert tortoise burrows underground for protection from the sun.

Below North America's zebra-tailed lizard runs with its banded tail curled forward. If a hawk grabs the tail, it falls off and the lizard escapes.

DESERTS OF AFRICA AND ASIA

Stony and sandy deserts sprawl from the Atlantic Ocean through northern Africa and into Asia. Africa's Sahara is the world's largest desert. The tropical deserts are hot by day, but cold at night. In the deserts of Central Asia the winters are bitterly cold.

All these deserts are homes to insects, scorpions, and spiders. Hard, waterproof "skins" stop their bodies from drying up. Many never drink. Beetles eat dry plants or dung. Locusts chew any leaves they can find. Huge swarms of locusts fly great distances to find new feeding grounds. Insects in the Sahara are eaten by long-eared desert hedgehogs and blunt-headed lizards called agamids. Snakes hunt these lizards and small rodents, such as jerboas. Jerboas and sand rats fall prey to the lanner falcon and the long-eared fennec fox.

Moving around is difficult in a soft, sandy desert. Some snakes slither along with a strange sideways movement called sidewinding. Shiny-bodied lizards with little legs can swim through sand.

Camels can last for days without eating or drinking. They store food in their hump, and their bodies save water by sweating only when the temperature soars very, very high.

Above Two tall kokerboom or "quiver trees" rise from the rocky floor of Namibia's Namib desert. This southwest African desert is one of the driest places on Earth. Green leaves are scarce in its bleak, bare wilderness.

Below Arabian camels cross a sandy waste. Padded toes stop them from sinking in soft sand. They can travel 100 miles (160 km) a day. Their main homes are the deserts of Asia and Africa.

Above These Namaqua sand grouse flew far across an African desert to find water. After drinking, they carry water in their breast feathers back to their young.

Right Jerboas bounce across hot sand on their long legs. They use their much shorter 'arms' for burrowing. These small rodents never need to drink. Plants give them all the moisture they need.

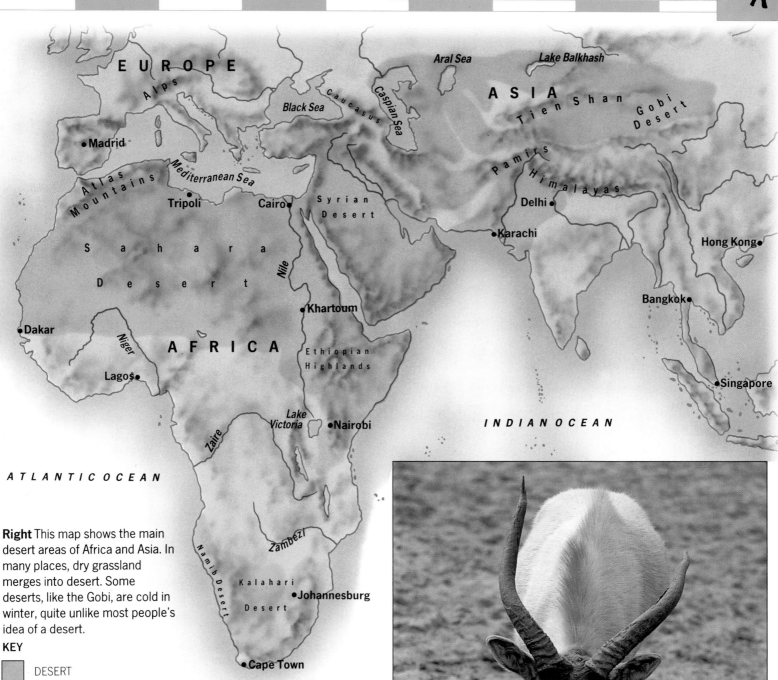

Right This map shows the main desert areas of Africa and Asia. In many places, dry grassland merges into desert. Some deserts, like the Gobi, are cold in winter, quite unlike most people's idea of a desert.

KEY

▨ DESERT

Sidewinder

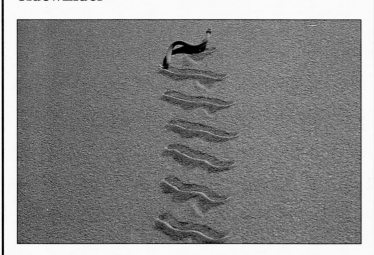

A viper sidewinds across a sandy desert, leaving tracks that look like the rungs of a ladder. Sidewinding snakes move by lifting different parts of the body off the ground in turn. This way, none of it rests on the burning hot sand for more than a moment. As soon as the sidewinder stops moving, it burrows quickly, to escape the desert heat.

Above Addax antelopes roam some of the harshest parts of Africa's Sahara Desert. They live where it is too hot and dry for almost any other creatures. Splayed hooves help them travel far across soft sand in search of food. They feed mainly on the leaves or seeds of grasses that spring up following a shower of rain. Addax antelopes drink water when they can, but they usually get enough moisture from the plants they eat.

RAIN FORESTS OF AMERICA

Halfway between the North and South poles lies the equator — an imaginary line around the middle of the Earth. Lands close to the equator are hot, and some are very rainy. This region is called the tropics.

Rain forests grow where it is hot and wet. The air and soil are always warm and moist, so trees can grow all year. Tropical rain forests hold more kinds of trees and animals than anywhere else in the world. Most creatures live high up in the bright, leafy canopy. Orchids and other plants perch there on branches, and creeping plants called lianas climb tree trunks to reach the sunshine. Lower down, shrubs, ferns, and fungi grow in the dim light of the forest floor.

Tropical rain forest covers parts of Central America and much of South America around the mighty river Amazon. Huge, bird-eating spiders and beetles as long as a person's hand live there, as well as tiny hummingbirds that are not much bigger than a bee. Frogs lay their eggs in tiny pools of rainwater formed in the leafy plants that grow on trees.

Sloths, monkeys, porcupines, and iguana lizards climb trees, gripping with their claws or tails. Macaws and toucans — colorful forest birds — use their big strong beaks to feed on tree fruits.

Jaguars, anaconda snakes, and harpy eagles are among the largest and most dangerous rain forest predators.

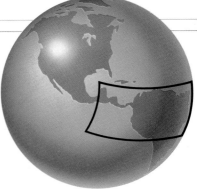

Above The jaguar is the strongest and largest cat of the American rain forest. Very large specimens weigh 300 lbs (135 kg). It kills deer, tapirs, and wild pigs.

Above Capuchin monkeys eat insects, fruits, and seeds. They climb high up among the trees in search of food. Like other American monkeys, a capuchin can grip the branches with its tail.

Right Plants grow on plants in the dimly lit, moist air of the Monteverde Cloud Forest Reserve in Central America. Twigs and branches drip with algae, lichens, mosses, bromeliads, ferns, and other epiphytes (plants that grow on other plants). Most take in nourishment from dead leaves that lie in crevices of bark. Even trees can use this extra food supply. High above the ground their trunks sprout roots that burrow in the rotting vegetation clinging to their branches.

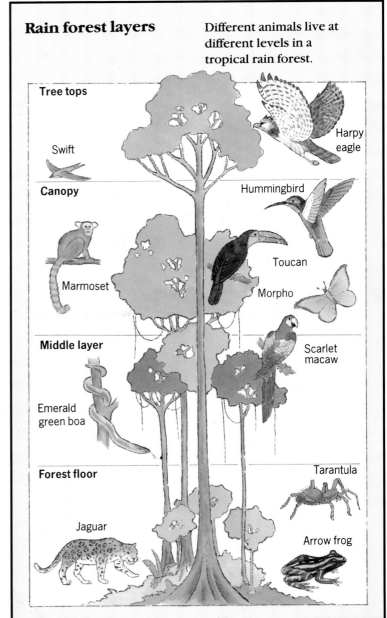

Rain forest layers

Different animals live at different levels in a tropical rain forest.

Tree tops
Swift
Harpy eagle

Canopy
Hummingbird
Toucan
Marmoset
Morpho

Middle layer
Scarlet macaw
Emerald green boa

Forest floor
Tarantula
Jaguar
Arrow frog

Sloth

A young three-toed sloth (above) hangs upside down, gripping branches with its hooklike claws. Green algae growing in their hair make them hard to see. Sloths spend almost all their lives in the trees. They creep from branch to branch, eating buds and leaves. They cling to branches so strongly that they can sleep without falling. Sloths move very slowly, and some may spend their whole life browsing in the same tree.

Forest butterflies

Forest butterflies with different colors fly at different levels. The colors help protect them. Butterflies with see-through wings (below left) are hard to see on the shady forest floor. Above the ground, striped, yellow and black zebra butterflies blend with flecks of sunlight. Higher still, birds find it difficult to follow bright blue (below right), red, and black butterflies flying in and out of light and shadow. Some butterflies are protected because they look like poisonous kinds that birds refuse to eat — even though they are not really poisonous.

Below Black and orange-red bands warn predators that this arrow poison frog is dangerous to eat. Indian hunters kill monkeys by poisoning arrow tips with juice from the frogs.

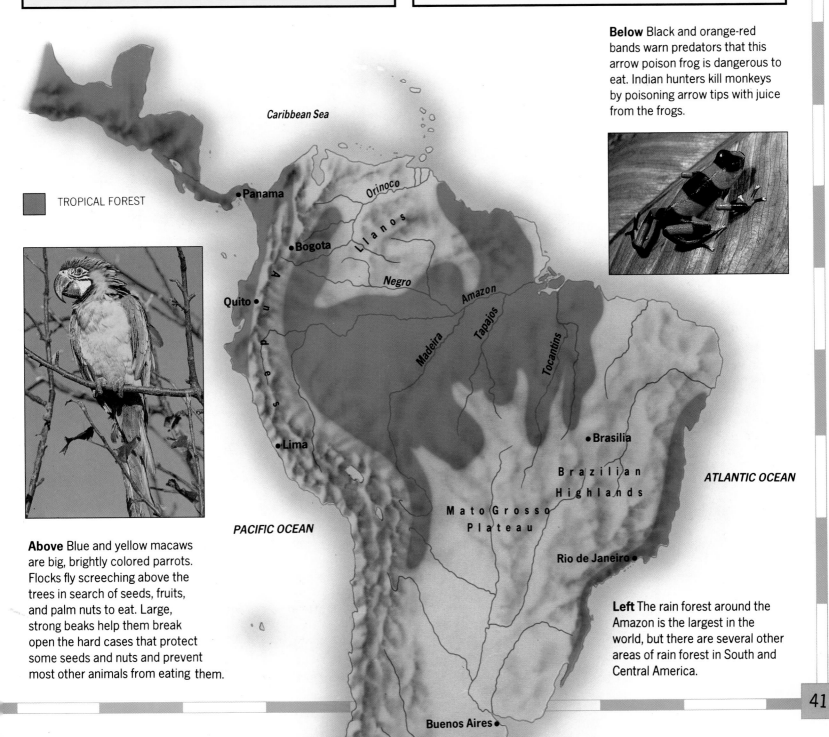

TROPICAL FOREST

Caribbean Sea

Panama

Orinoco

Llanos

Bogota

Negro

Quito

Amazon

Madeira

Tapajos

Tocantins

Andes

Lima

Brasilia

Brazilian Highlands

ATLANTIC OCEAN

Mato Grosso Plateau

PACIFIC OCEAN

Rio de Janeiro

Buenos Aires

Above Blue and yellow macaws are big, brightly colored parrots. Flocks fly screeching above the trees in search of seeds, fruits, and palm nuts to eat. Large, strong beaks help them break open the hard cases that protect some seeds and nuts and prevent most other animals from eating them.

Left The rain forest around the Amazon is the largest in the world, but there are several other areas of rain forest in South and Central America.

AFRICAN FORESTS

Tropical rain forest covers parts of West and Central Africa – though much of it has been chopped down. Just as in South America there is always plenty to eat and it is always warm, so some kinds of cold-blooded animals are able to grow extra large in the rain forest. Some mantid insects are big enough to eat small lizards. Driver ant soldiers with huge jaws can kill almost any small animal they meet. There are giant goliath frogs that can swallow mice.

Many of the forest animals are camouflaged. Green tree snakes match the colors of living leaves. Bongo antelopes and genets (catlike hunters) have stripes or spots like splashes of sunlight shining on dark ground. Until they move, these creatures seem invisible.

The most brightly colored forest animals are butterflies and birds such as the Congo peafowl, touracos, and pittas.

Africa's forests hold our closest living relatives, the chimpanzees and gorillas. Both great apes live in groups. Gorillas usually eat leaves, roots, and bark. Chimpanzees enjoy fruit, but some eat termites too. Gangs of chimpanzees will even catch and kill wild pigs and monkeys. Chimpanzees and gorillas sleep in trees on platforms made by bending leafy branches.

Above Tropical rain forest is just one of several kinds of forests found in Africa. This strange mountain forest is in East Africa. Its tall plants include giant types of herbs and shrubs that are often grown as garden plants.

Above Gaboon vipers grow more than 5 ft (1.5 m) long. They are almost impossible to see among the dead leaves on the forest floor. They hide in places where they know rodents will pass, and spring out and strike them with their poisoned fangs.

Gorillas

Our near relatives the gorillas are the world's largest, strongest apes. A wild adult male can weigh three times as much as a person, but the females are much smaller. These great apes usually walk on all fours. Smaller ones climb trees. Gorillas live in family troops made up of a large male, several females, and some young. The troop eats plants as it slowly wanders through a stretch of forest a few miles across.

There are two main groups of gorillas. Lowland gorillas live in west-central Africa. Mountain gorillas live farther east in moist mountain forests in more eastern-central Africa. All lead peaceful lives, though a big male may threaten a leopard or a person. Mountain gorillas will even let people sit with them, once they are sure they mean no harm.

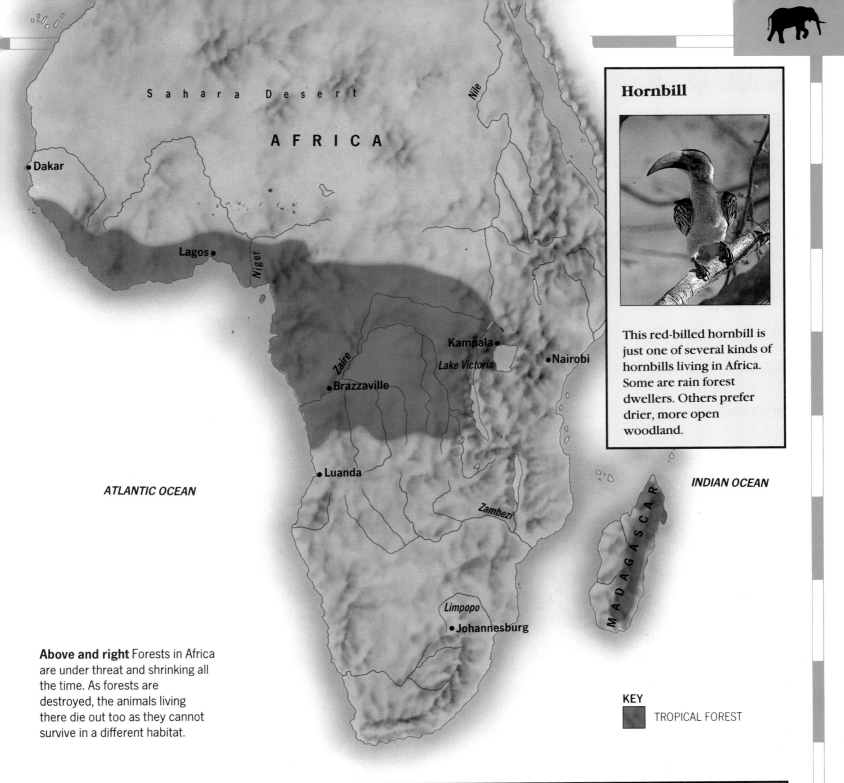

S a h a r a   D e s e r t

Nile

A F R I C A

• Dakar

Lagos •

Niger

Zaïre

Kampala •

Lake Victoria

• Nairobi

• Brazzaville

ATLANTIC OCEAN

• Luanda

Zambezi

INDIAN OCEAN

MADAGASCAR

Limpopo

• Johannesburg

Hornbill

This red-billed hornbill is just one of several kinds of hornbills living in Africa. Some are rain forest dwellers. Others prefer drier, more open woodland.

Above and right Forests in Africa are under threat and shrinking all the time. As forests are destroyed, the animals living there die out too as they cannot survive in a different habitat.

KEY

▮ TROPICAL FOREST

Madagascar

Madagascar is a long, hot island nation. Many millions of years ago, Madagascar was joined to Africa. The types of animals living there now are survivors from that time. Their ancestors were cut off from mainland Africa when Madagascar became an island. Nine out of ten of Madagascar's animal species live nowhere else.

Several kinds of unusual tortoises live there as well as three-quarters of the world's known species of chameleons.

Madagascar is the only home of some strange, small mammals called tenrecs. Some are prickly like hedgehogs. Some have pointed heads like shrews.

Only on Madagascar or nearby islands will you see creatures like the ring-tailed lemur (right). There are about two dozen different kinds of these fluffy, long-tailed relatives of monkeys. The smallest lemur is no bigger than a large mouse. The strangest is the squirrel-like aye-aye, which uses a long thin middle finger to pull grubs from holes in wood. Lemurs and tenrecs are sometimes eaten by a catlike hunter called the fossa.

ANIMALS OF SOUTHERN ASIA

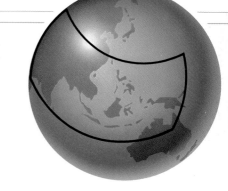

Millions of people farm the land in southern Asia, but there are still forests, deserts, and grasslands where wild animals roam.

Some creatures came from outside the area. Jackals, Asiatic lions, and gazelles moved across from deserts to the west. Tigers came to southern Asia from the east.

Most animals of India have their homes among the teak trees and tall bamboo grasses of the Deccan Plateau. There are large plant eaters — sambar deer and wild gaur cattle. Langur monkeys live among the trees. Porcupines, lizards, tortoises, and snakes live on the forest floor.

Leopards, tigers, and Indian hunting dogs are India's big-game hunters. Sloth bears look terrifying but are not — they eat termites. Antelopes live in open land, while the moist forests of the Deccan have water buffalo, swamp deer, and elephants. The Indian rhinoceros is threatened by poachers and by the destruction of its natural habitat.

Farther east there are hot, steamy forests. These are home to many monkeys and their relatives, including tiny tarsiers and big, heavy orangutans, the largest apes in Asia.

There are lizards, snakes, and frogs that can almost fly. They stretch out skin "parachutes" or "wings" as they glide from tree to tree. The best glider is probably the colugo, a squirrel-like mammal with a web of skin between its arms, legs, and tail.

Forest giants of this area include stick insects that grow up to twelve inches (thirty centimeters) long.

Above Tall trees along a forest road in Sri Lanka. Various broad-leaved trees grow in parts of southern Asia. Evergreens thrive where it is always moist, but trees that shed their leaves can grow where there is a long dry season.

Left Weaver ants use their young to help build nests from leaves. First several worker ants pull the edges of two leaves together. Then other workers grasp larvae in their jaws and move them between both leaves. The larvae spin a kind of silk that glues the edges of the leaves together.

Orangutans

The orangutan is the largest Asian ape. Its name means 'man of the woods,' and it lives in the tropical rain forests of southern Asia. Long arms and short legs make it better at swinging through trees than walking on the ground. But an orangutan can walk upright along a branch if it holds a branch above it to keep its balance. It spends much of the day eating fruit, leaves, shoots, and bark. At night it sleeps in a nest built in a tree fork high off the ground.

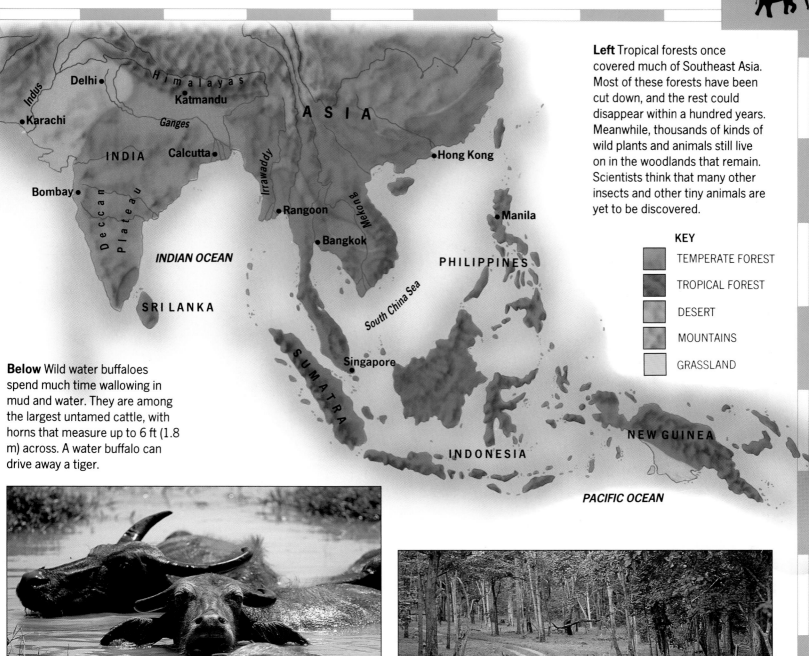

Left Tropical forests once covered much of Southeast Asia. Most of these forests have been cut down, and the rest could disappear within a hundred years. Meanwhile, thousands of kinds of wild plants and animals still live on in the woodlands that remain. Scientists think that many other insects and other tiny animals are yet to be discovered.

KEY

■	TEMPERATE FOREST
■	TROPICAL FOREST
■	DESERT
■	MOUNTAINS
■	GRASSLAND

Below Wild water buffaloes spend much time wallowing in mud and water. They are among the largest untamed cattle, with horns that measure up to 6 ft (1.8 m) across. A water buffalo can drive away a tiger.

Above Some gaur and their young cross a woodland track. Small herds of these wild cattle live on rocky, wooded hills in Southeast Asia. Males are up to 6 ft (1.8 m) high at the shoulder and weigh about a ton (1,000 kg).

Left Tigers are the largest of the big cats. A large adult male can weigh as much as three people. Black stripes on a reddish coat camouflage tigers as they prowl through woodland or tall grass. They will eat frogs and tortoises, but they prefer big meaty beasts such as deer, wild cattle, and wild pigs. They creep up on their prey, then suddenly rush and seize it by the neck.

ANIMALS OF AUSTRALIA

As the Earth's continents shift, parts break away. Millions of years ago, Australia became separated from other landmasses. Australian animals were cut off from the rest of the world and evolved in their own ways. There are many animal groups that are only found in Australia and New Guinea.

Australia is home to most of the world's pouched mammals or marsupials. These mostly died out on other continents, because they were not able to compete well for food with the placentals. (Placentals are mammals without pouches found just about everywhere else.) Kangaroos, wombats, and koalas are all marsupials.

Australian mammals and birds mostly live among the woods and grasslands around the moister edges of the continent.

Deep inland lie huge deserts where there are reptiles such as the thorny devil, a very prickly lizard. There is the frilled lizard, too, that spreads a skin umbrella to scare off enemies. Desert predators include some of the most poisonous snakes in the world.

Perhaps the strangest desert animals are the moisture-loving frogs. Wrapped in waterproof material, rather like plastic bags, they can doze underground for years until rain fills the shallow pools where they will breed.

Above The red kangaroo is one of Australia's largest kinds of kangaroo. It is as big as a tall person and can jump as far as 26 ft (8 m) to clear a fence or fallen tree. Herds graze on grassy plains.

Above Koalas live high up in eucalyptus trees. They are fussy eaters that eat only eucalyptus leaves. Because of this they smell of eucalyptus – a bit like cough drops.

Marsupials

When a young marsupial is born, it is very underdeveloped. It leaves its mother's womb when it is only a few inches long and manages to crawl up through her fur into her pouch. There, it fixes its mouth firmly onto her teat and feeds on milk from her body. Gradually, it develops until it can peep out of the pouch, then make short trips outside, and, finally, leave its mother's body altogether.

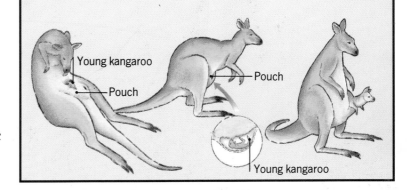

Young kangaroo

Pouch

Pouch

Young kangaroo

Animal lookalikes

Many marsupials look like placental mammals found in other countries. They are not related to them – they have simply adapted to the same sort of life. The marsupial mouse (right) lives in eucalyptus forests.

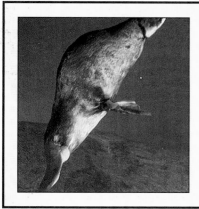

Egg-laying mammals

Two very strange mammals of Australia are the echidna (right) and platypus (left). Both are egg-laying mammals, or monotremes.

The platypus is about 20 in (50 cm) long, with webbed feet. It swims in streams, scooping up worms and shellfish with its beak. The female lays her soft-shelled eggs in a tunnel in a riverbank. She keeps them warm until they hatch and then feeds the young milk from her body.

The echidna also lays eggs, but in other ways it is very unlike the platypus. It is spiny and eats termites.

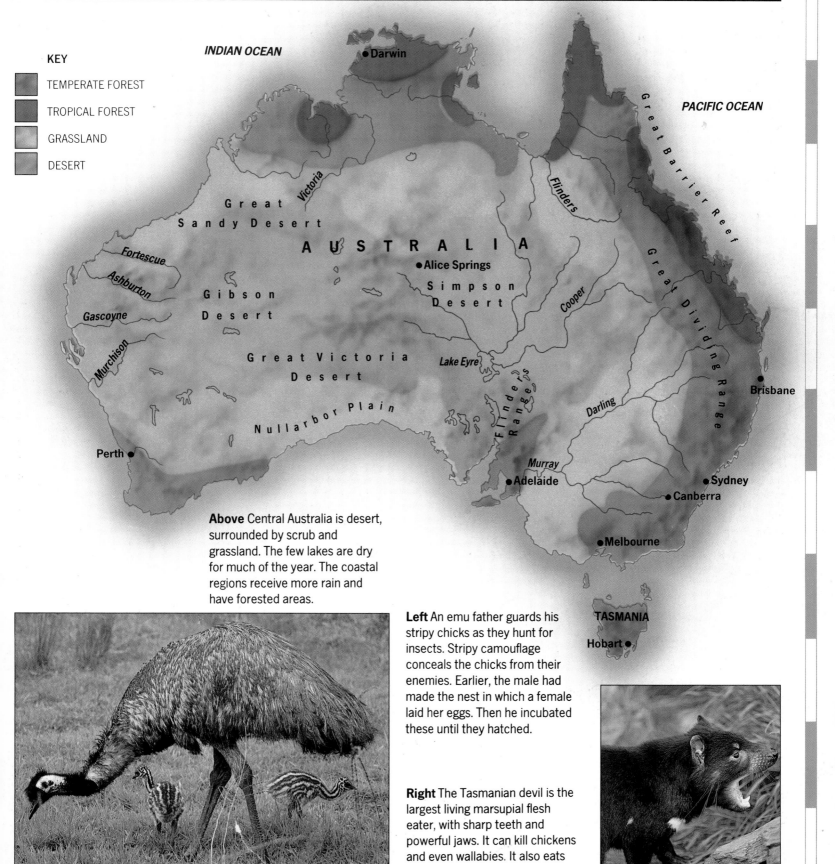

KEY

- TEMPERATE FOREST
- TROPICAL FOREST
- GRASSLAND
- DESERT

INDIAN OCEAN

• Darwin

PACIFIC OCEAN

Victoria

Great
Sandy Desert

A U S T R A L I A

Flinders

Fortescue

Ashburton

• Alice Springs

Simpson
Desert

Cooper

G i b s o n
D e s e r t

Gascoyne

Murchison

Great Victoria
Desert

Lake Eyre

Flinders Ranges

Great Barrier Reef

Great Dividing Range

• Brisbane

Darling

Nullarbor Plain

Perth •

Murray

• Adelaide

• Sydney
• Canberra

• Melbourne

Above Central Australia is desert, surrounded by scrub and grassland. The few lakes are dry for much of the year. The coastal regions receive more rain and have forested areas.

TASMANIA

Hobart •

Left An emu father guards his stripy chicks as they hunt for insects. Stripy camouflage conceals the chicks from their enemies. Earlier, the male had made the nest in which a female laid her eggs. Then he incubated these until they hatched.

Right The Tasmanian devil is the largest living marsupial flesh eater, with sharp teeth and powerful jaws. It can kill chickens and even wallabies. It also eats any dead animals it finds.

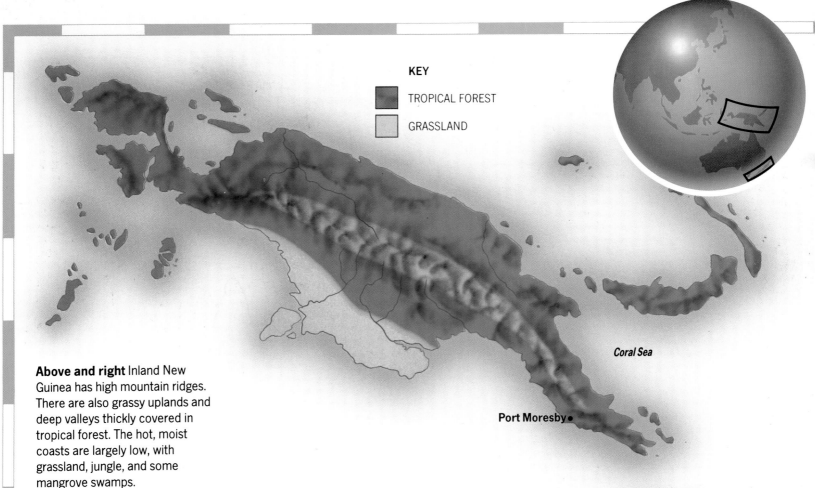

KEY

■ TROPICAL FOREST

☐ GRASSLAND

Coral Sea

Port Moresby ●

Above and right Inland New Guinea has high mountain ridges. There are also grassy uplands and deep valleys thickly covered in tropical forest. The hot, moist coasts are largely low, with grassland, jungle, and some mangrove swamps.

NEW GUINEA AND NEW ZEALAND

The large tropical island of New Guinea lies off northern Australia. Well to the southeast of Australia stand the lonelier and much cooler islands of New Zealand. New Guinea and New Zealand both have some remarkable animals.

In New Guinea's mountain forests male birds of paradise perch or hang from branches to show off long, brilliantly colored feathers to the drab females. On the ground, male bower-birds build little huts for female bowerbirds to admire, and big flightless birds called cassowaries roam the forest floor. Tree kangaroos climb branches high above in search of leaves to eat. A scared tree kangaroo can drop forty feet (twelve meters) and land safely.

New Zealand's only native mammals are two kinds of bats (though there are plenty of other mammals that people brought with them when they settled there). With no mammal enemies to fear, some New Zealand birds evolved to lose the use of their wings. These ground birds include the kiwi, takahe, weka, and kakapo, a flightless parrot. There are even flightless crickets, called wetas.

Right The blossom bat belongs to a group of tropical bats that feed on flowers. The bats take nectar and pollen. As they do so, they accidentally spread pollen onto other flowers that they visit. This pollinates the flowers so these produce seeds.

Below A male bird of paradise displays to win a mate, showing off his fine feathers to their best advantage. Usually a group of males display close together to impress some females. The females are quite drably colored.

Life in hot water

New Zealand's North Island has many hot springs and streams where some creatures live, but where it is too hot for most water animals. Dragonfly larvae, snails, and fish called carp all thrive in streams at 85°F to 95°F (30°C to 35°C). Water beetles, roundworms, and tiny organisms called rotifers survive at 95°F to 110°F (35°C to 45°C). Bacteria and algae can survive in water that is almost boiling.

Above A tuatara. Animals like this were around at the time of the dinosaurs. They survived because New Zealand was cut off from the rest of the world and there were no animals to hunt them.

Above The brown kiwi is a wingless, tailless, hairy-looking bird no bigger than a chicken. Like some other New Zealand birds, kiwis cannot fly. They feed on insects, worms, and berries, sniffing them out with nostrils at the tip of their long beak. They live in dense, moist forests, hunting by night, hiding by day.

Left New Zealand is mainly two big islands. North Island includes volcanic mountains, rugged hills, forests, and long, sandy beaches. South Island has flat grassy plains, rolling hills, and mountains. In the far south are forests, snowy peaks, and glaciers.

Tasman Sea

•Auckland

•Hamilton

N O R T H   I S L A N D

Lake Taupo

Nelson•

•Wellington

S o u t h e r n   A l p s

•Christchurch

S O U T H
I S L A N D

Dunedin•

KEY

 TEMPERATE FOREST

 GRASSLAND

SECTION 3: WATER LIFE

Two thirds of the Earth's surface is covered by water — mostly seas and oceans, but also rivers, streams, lakes, and ponds. A variety of animals spend all their lives in or near water and, like land animals, they are adapted to live in different places and in different climates.

RIVER LIFE

River life is different in different parts of the world — and it is different in different parts of a river. Many rivers rise in the mountains. As the cool clear water rushes quickly downhill, water animals risk being washed away. Some, such as young mayflies, hide under stones and firmly grip the riverbed. Fish that live in this part of a river must be able to swim against a strong current.

As the current slows, different kinds of fish and insects can make their home in the river. By the time it reaches the lowlands, the river is slow, deep, broad, and muddy — and full of living things.

Tropical rivers, such as the Nile and Amazon, are always warm and teem with fish, reptiles, and amphibians. Some grow astonishingly large. Africa's Nile perch, South America's arapaima, and the Pa beuk catfish from Southeast Asia are among the largest freshwater fish on Earth. All can grow heavier than a person. In South America, gigantic arrau turtles bask on islets in the Amazon.

The world's biggest reptiles — alligators, crocodiles, and gharials — all swim in the rivers of the tropics.

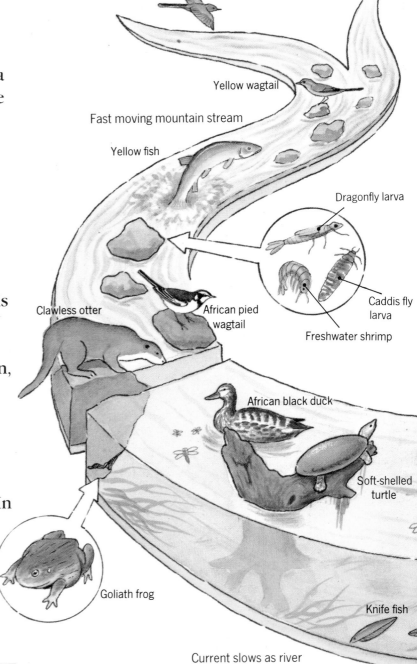

Wagtail

Yellow wagtail

Fast moving mountain stream

Yellow fish

Dragonfly larva

Caddis fly larva

Freshwater shrimp

Clawless otter

African pied wagtail

African black duck

Soft-shelled turtle

Goliath frog

Knife fish

Current slows as river reaches lowlands

Right A damselfly rests on a water crowfoot flower. This lovely insect began life as a rather ugly creature living under water. Full grown, it climbed out, split its skin, spread its wings, and fluttered away.

Above This imaginary scene shows some of the animals living in or beside a tropical African river. (No single river is likely to contain all these.) Small underwater creatures include freshwater shrimps, dragonfly larvae, and caddis-fly larvae. Adult dragonflies are pictured darting here and there above the surface.

Some of these invertebrates get eaten by small river fish. African river fish include knife fish, cichlids, yellow fish, *Tilapia*, and lungfish. The Nile perch is a big, fierce predator that eats fish smaller than itself. Africa's amphibians include the clawed toad, which spends its life in water, and the rare goliath frog,

50

Locating prey

Fish that usually live in muddy water cannot rely on their eyes to find food. Africa's upside-down catfish (shown here the right way up) has long 'whiskers' to help it feel for food. Africa's elephant snout fish and South America's electric eel both surround themselves with an invisible electric field and locate any fish that swim within it. The electric eel can even kill fish with a powerful electric surge.

Above A Mississippi alligator lurks on a riverbank in southeastern North America.

Right Otters of various kinds live along rivers on most continents. They are agile swimmers.

Darter
Sand grouse
Pied kingfisher
Osprey
Crocodile
Dragonfly
Tilapia
Red-billed duck
Hippopotamus
Great white egret
Clawed toad
Cichlids
Tilapia
Nile perch
Lungfish

Near the sea the river is deep, broad, and slow-moving

the largest frog on Earth. The soft-shelled turtle and the Nile crocodile are both reptiles. The hippopotamus is the world's largest freshwater mammal. The picture also shows nine kinds of birds. The African black duck and red-billed duck are shown swimming on the water. The darter and kingfisher plunge below the surface to hunt fish, while the osprey swoops down to scoop fish from the river. Some egrets and their relatives the herons spear fish with their beaks. Both wagtails catch water insects or others living by the water's edge. Sand grouse may fly many miles from a desert to reach a river for their daily drink.

LAKES AND MARSHES

The still waters of lowland lakes, ponds, and marshes hold more kinds of animals than almost any other places. People cross the world to admire the splendid wildlife of Africa's Okavango Swamp, Florida's Everglades, and France's Camargue.

In mild climates, frogs lay their eggs in still, shallow water. In spring this soon warms up and helps the eggs hatch into tadpoles. Some tadpoles in turn form food for fish, newts, and water snakes. Frogs, newts, and snakes are snapped up by storks and herons – birds with long, pointed beaks.

In the rainy season, some tropical rivers may overflow their banks to form huge lakes on either side. Then fish invade the land and feed on tree fruits falling in the water. As the floods go down, the fish must find their way back into the shrinking river.

In the dry season, shallow tropical pools dry up and most fish die. First, though, they lay eggs in the mud. The eggs hatch after rain refills their ponds.

A frog's life

In spring, the females of these European frogs lay their eggs in ponds. The males fertilize the eggs, which remain in the water as blobs of jelly, with a tiny creature developing inside each of them.

Eventually, black tadpoles emerge from the spawn. A young tadpole has feathery gills at the side of its head and a long tail, which it uses for swimming. It remains in the water all the time, breathing through its gills. As the tadpole grows, the gills vanish, small limbs appear, and the tail slowly shrinks. When the young frog has formed, it can breathe through lungs and live in the open air. It is ready to leave the water.

This pattern is similar among many other amphibians. The same kind of ponds that frogs use to breed are also homes for the tadpoles of many different species, or kinds, of newts and toads.

Above Hippopotamuses graze on land at night but spend most of the day in the water, munching water cabbage. Their droppings fertilize the water plants. These plants then form food for water snails and fish, which in turn are gobbled up by storks, fish eagles, pelicans, and other birds. Hippopotamuses live in slow-moving rivers as well as in lakes.

Below Viperine snakes swim in the weedy pools and rivers of southwestern Europe and northwestern Africa. They hunt frogs, newts, and fish. Some have a zigzag pattern like a viper's, but they are not poisonous.

ARCTIC OCEAN

Great Bear Lake
Great Slave Lake

Lake Winnipeg

NORTH AMERICA

Lake Superior
Lake Michigan

Lake Huron
Lake Ontario
Lake Erie

Everglades

ATLANTIC OCEAN

Caribbean Sea

SOUTH
AMERICA

Lake Titicaca

EUROPE

ASIA

Lake Baikal

Lake Balkhash

Camargue

PACIFIC OCEAN

AFRICA

Lake Chad

Lake Volta

Lake Victoria
Lake Tanganyika
Lake Malawi

INDIAN
OCEAN

Okavango Swamp

AUSTRALIA

Lake Eyre

Above The largest freshwater lakes lie in North America and Africa. The deepest lake is Lake Baikal in Asia. The Baikal seal and nearly 1,000 other kinds of animals live only there.

Right Flamingoes feeding in the warm waters of an East African lake. The birds use their beaks to filter billions of tiny organisms from the water to eat.

Below Male and female Siamese fighting fishes. These fish live in ponds and flooded rice fields in southern Asia. They can breathe air at the surface, so they can survive in polluted ponds where most fish would suffocate.

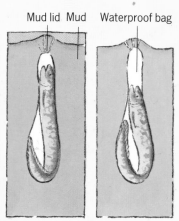

Water

Mud lid Mud   Waterproof bag

Lungfish

Lungfish survival

This African lungfish lives in swampy waters that disappear in the dry season. As the water dries up, the lungfish dives into the mud underwater. Its body produces slimy mucus that hardens into a waterproof bag to stop it from drying up. A mud lid lets in air for the fish to breathe with its lung-like swim bladder. When rain refills the swamp, it swims away.

SANDY SHORES

Many creatures live on sandy shores all over the world. Different creatures live on different parts of the beach. High up, there may be rotting seaweed, which provides food for beetles, seaweed fly maggots, tiny worms, and sand-hoppers. Farther down, where the water rises and falls with the tide, many animals burrow beneath the surface when the tide is out. The sand there stays comfortably damp and never grows too hot or cold.

When the tide comes in, crabs, shrimps, and hidden fish come up to eat. But most worms and shellfish stay buried. Some push up little tubes that suck in water containing tiny living things. Others put out tentacles that grope around for scraps. Low down on the beach live moisture-loving flatfish, sand eels, and starfish.

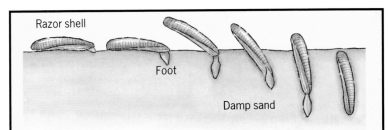

Razor shell

Foot

Damp sand

Burrowers in the sand

Razor shells live in a pair of long, narrow shells, a bit like old-fashioned razors. The razor shell uses a long, fleshy foot to bury itself. It pushes this into the sand, where the tip swells to make a kind of anchor. It uses this to pull itself down. It does this several times, very fast. Within a minute the razor shell is beneath the sand. When the tide comes in, the buried animal sucks in food and water through a tube.

Right A heart urchin, burrowing into the beach.

Above A spiny cockle has opened its shell and begun to burrow with its muscular foot.

Mermaid's purse

Worm casts

Shore crab

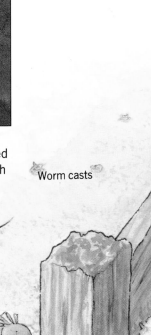

Razor shell

Shore crab

Starfish

Herring gull

Razor shell

Tube worms

Sand eels

Plaice

Below Like other flatfish, this topknot camouflages itself and lies on the seabed.

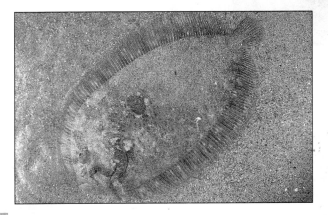

Above The large illustration shows creatures to be seen on sandy and rocky shores in many northern regions of the world.

On the sandy beach, the mermaid's purse is a dogfish egg case, washed up by the tide. A dead starfish and the empty shells of some dead razor shells also lie on the sand. Two shore crabs have scuttled from damp hiding places, and a herring gull patrols the beach to feed on any tidbits it can find. Lower down the shore, tube worms hide in their stiff tubes, which poke from beneath the sand. At high tide these worms will push out tentacles to trap food particles. Sand eels buried in the sand will swim out as the sea comes in, and plaice will start feeding.

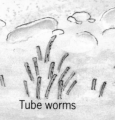

ROCKY SHORES

Rocky shores are difficult, dangerous places for animals to live. The rocks are beaten by the sea and dried by the wind. They are baked by the sun and frozen in winter. Yet creatures survive there. Some, such as barnacles and limpets, cling to the rocks so closely that the waves cannot tear them away. Their shells protect them from the drying wind and sun – and predators.

Rock pools are safer. Deep rock pools never dry up or get too hot or cold. These places are homes for such animals as crabs, shrimps, sponges, and small fish. Many squeeze into crevices when storm waves come – this saves them from being bashed against the rocks.

Despite their dangers, rocky shores provide good feeding grounds. Limpets, topshells, and sea urchins nibble slimy algae growing on the rocks. Barnacles trap tiny particles of food in water. Crabs, worms, and certain shellfish eat food scraps lying on the shore. In turn, these small shore creatures form food for carnivorous sea snails, starfish, fish, gulls, and even people.

Left A huge nesting colony of gannets covers much of this rocky island. Steep cliffs and the sea protect nesting seabirds from most enemies.

Right Some animals in rock pools are as bright as jewels. Among those pictured are a starfish, sea urchins, and sea anemones.

Barnacles

Sea anemone

Prawn

Periwinkle

Brittle star

Goby

Limpet

Starfish

Mussels

Below Sea lions on a rocky shore in the Galápagos Islands, off the Pacific coast of South America.

This rocky shore shows some of the different kinds of creatures living in or near a rock pool left when the tide went out. In the pool, the goby, prawns, sea anemone, and brittle star can move around and feed as well as if the tide were in. Unless the starfish crawls into the pool soon, it will dry up and die. Outside the pool, shellfish such as barnacles, limpets, mussels, and periwinkles can withstand hours of dry air and hot sunshine. These creatures close their shells tightly to keep their bodies inside moist. When the tide comes in, barnacles put out feathery "arms" to trap food particles. Mussels suck these in through fleshy tubes. Limpets and periwinkles graze on algae on the rocks.

SALT MARSHES

Salt marshes are low, muddy shores. They lie around the coast of much of North America, northwestern Europe, southeastern South America, and other continents. Here rivers have washed mud into the sea, building a soft, thick carpet. Inshore, low plants cover mudbanks that peep above the water. Between these banks lie deep, narrow creeks. At low tide you can see the muddy floors of the creeks and the bare mud covering the seabed farther out. Near river mouths, the water is fresh when the tide is out and salty when it is in.

The mud is home for billions of tiny burrowing worms, snails, and shrimps. Most kinds would be suffocated by the mud, or killed when the water changes from fresh to salty. The mud burrowers have, however, solved these problems. Some shellfish, for example, breathe through tubes sticking up through the mud and shut their shells when the water changes from fresh to salty.

At high tide many of the burrowers come out to feed. Then crabs, shrimps, and fish such as skate and mullet swim or crawl inshore to hunt or browse on scraps. Some of these hunters in turn fall prey to seals or diving seabirds.

At low tide, flocks of long-legged wading birds poke their slim beaks deep down to capture worms and snails.

Long and short beaks

Waders find food by poking their beaks into the mud. What they find depends on how long their beaks are. Birds like the knot, ringed plover, and sanderling can only reach those shellfish and sandhoppers that burrow just below the surface. The redshank, with its longer beak, can reach worms and other shellfish that burrow deeper. Godwits and curlews, with even longer beaks, can reach deeper still. Because they eat different foods, there is enough for all.

Below This diagram shows how birds with beaks of different lengths can reach different creatures below the surface of the mud.

Above A black-winged stilt's very long legs and long beak enable it to find food that other wading birds cannot reach.

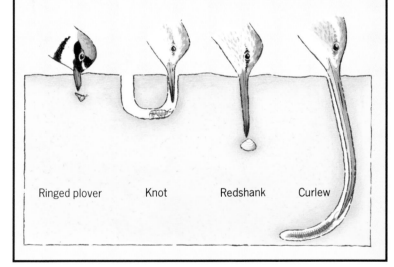

Ringed plover   Knot   Redshank   Curlew

Left The underside of a sea mouse (a kind of worm), showing its body segments. Bristles, like hairs, on its back gave it its name.

Below *Hydrobia* snails grow no bigger than a grain of wheat. As many as 40,000 may live in a square yard (meter) of mud.

Right Low down, close to the sea, the salt marsh is at its wettest. Flocks of birds like these knots hunt for food in the wet mud. Higher up, where the ground is drier, geese will graze on grasses and other plants.

ARCTIC OCEAN

NORTH AMERICA

EUROPE

ASIA

ATLANTIC OCEAN

Mediterranean Sea

PACIFIC OCEAN

Caribbean Sea

AFRICA

PACIFIC OCEAN

SOUTH AMERICA

INDIAN OCEAN

AUSTRALIA

Right Salt marshes are found in the coastal regions shown on this map. Many are rich in wildlife. Salt marshes are important breeding areas for fish and shellfish and are home to many birds.

Left At low tide we can see the muddy banks of the creeks in a salt marsh. The creeks fill with water at high tide, so only salt-resistant plants can grow here.

Above The peacock worm lives in a tube poking up from the mud low on the shore. At high tide the worm puts out a fan of tentacles to trap the food scraps drifting by.

MANGROVE SWAMPS

More than half of all tropical shores are made up of mangrove swamps. Mangroves are trees that have developed to survive in muddy waters. There are many different species of mangrove trees, but they all send out strange, tangled roots that show above the surface of the mud until the tide comes in to cover them. Huge numbers of animals find food and shelter among the mangroves.

Barnacles and oysters cling to the tree roots. Ants and crabs live in burrows in the mud between the roots. As the sea comes in, some ants and crabs can close their burrows. They survive by breathing the air inside until the sea goes out again.

Crabs share the mud with lobsters, prawns, and mudskippers — small, pop-eyed fish that skip along on wet mud in search of food. Archer fish swim among the roots and squirt a jet of water to bring down insects overhead.

While these water creatures find their food on land, wild cats and other land animals hunt in or by the water. Along the tropical shores of Southeast Asia, frogs, snakes, and monkeys look for crabs to eat when the tide is out. In South America there are crab-eating raccoons.

Above A mangrove swamp in Southeast Asia. Mangrove swamps teem with tiny creatures that eat the fallen and decaying mangrove leaves. These, in turn, attract crabs and shrimps, which are food for fish. Local fishermen, in turn, depend on catching fish and shrimps in the mangroves.

Below The scarlet ibis lives among the mangrove swamps of northeast South America. Its brilliant color comes from the reddish shrimps it eats. In zoos, these birds turn pale unless their food includes a special coloring. Like all ibises, these have a long neck, long, thin, downcurved beak, and long legs.

Above Fiddler crabs in the mangrove swamps of Southeast Asia. These three different crabs are just a few of the many shellfish living in the mangrove swamps. They are food for many animals — birds and even certain kinds of monkeys, such as the crab-eating macaque.

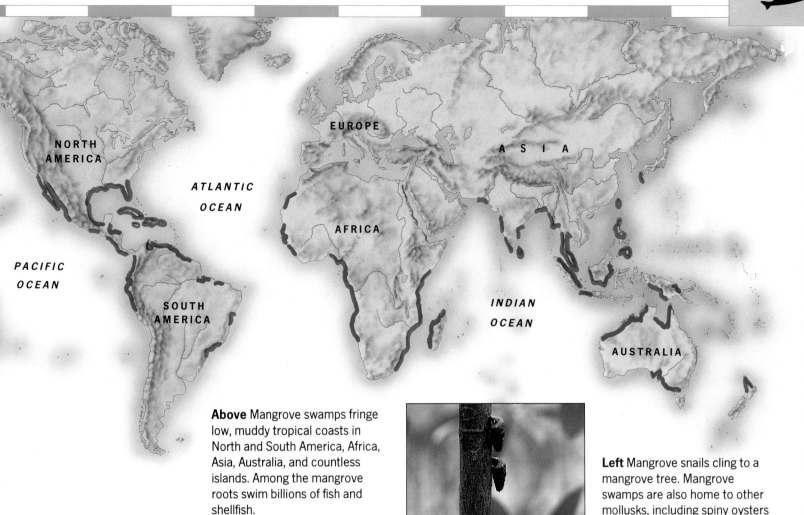

Above Mangrove swamps fringe low, muddy tropical coasts in North and South America, Africa, Asia, Australia, and countless islands. Among the mangrove roots swim billions of fish and shellfish.

Left Mangrove snails cling to a mangrove tree. Mangrove swamps are also home to other mollusks, including spiny oysters and periwinkles. Such shellfish often become meals for egrets, ibises, and other birds.

Below These macaque monkeys live in a mangrove forest in Southeast Asia. Some mangrove forest monkeys eat leaves and seldom leave the trees. Others eat shellfish and often swim.

Mudskippers

Mudskippers are small fish that can walk, skip around, and breathe, all out of the water. They have big eyes on top of their head, to watch for danger. On land, mudskippers push themselves along on fleshy fins that look a bit like arms. Some can even climb tree trunks by using special fins as suckers. Mudskippers can breathe some ordinary air, but they must carry water in chambers in their gills. They also splash themselves to keep their bodies moist. In a Southeast Asian mangrove swamp, one kind of mudskipper lives in very wet mud. Another lives on firmer mud, and others live farther up the shore. Some eat algae and some eat little animals. Others feed on animals and plants.

CORAL REEFS

In the warm, clear waters of the tropics, we find coral. Coral is hard – like rock – but is actually made up from the bodies of billions of tiny animals. These are the coral polyps. Each one lives inside a little coral cup. As some polyps die, others build new cups on top of old ones. So coral keeps growing up toward the surface of the sea.

Coral reefs are home to brightly colored shrimps, sea anemones, starfish, sea slugs, and sea worms. The reefs also teem with brilliantly colored triggerfish, surgeonfish, damselfish, and others.

Reef creatures produce millions of eggs and young, many of which are gobbled up by other reef creatures. Big fish such as sharks and groupers prey on smaller kinds that lurk among the coral or swim in shoals for safety.

Coral polyps themselves often end up eaten. Butterfly fish nibble them one by one, and parrotfish with jaws like parrots' beaks bite off whole coral chunks and crunch them up. Even dead coral gets attacked. Sea snails, date mussels, and palolo worms all burrow into it. In time all this damage helps to break up the coral reefs.

Clown fish and anemones

Clown fish swim unharmed among the tentacles of a big sea anemone. The anemone will attack most fish, firing off paralyzing stings. But clown fish wear some of the sea anemone's own sticky mucus, so it mistakes them for part of itself. The clown fish stay with the anemone. Their enemies – afraid of being hurt – stay away.

How atolls form

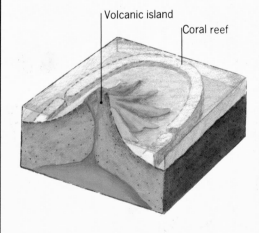

Volcanic island
Coral reef

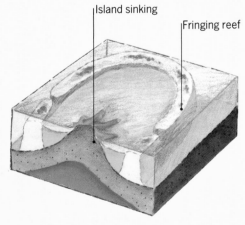

Island sinking
Fringing reef

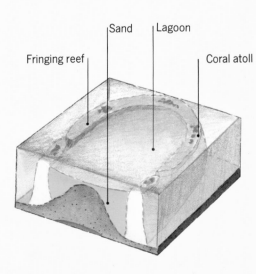

Sand | Lagoon
Fringing reef
Coral atoll

Coral atolls are islands of coral. Often, they are made up of a ring of small islands. Each coral atoll began as a coral reef fringing an island volcano. Gradually, over millions of years, the volcano sank beneath the sea as the rest of the Earth changed and the seas rose. But coral polyps built the reef upward as fast as the volcano went down. They kept on growing, just below the surface. In time the volcano disappeared below the waves, but the ring-shaped reef remained. Storm waves threw scraps of broken coral on top, and the reef became a ring of narrow, sandy islands just peeping above the sea. In the middle, where the volcano once stood, now lies a calm pool of seawater called a lagoon. Scores of coral atolls stand in the southwestern Pacific Ocean.

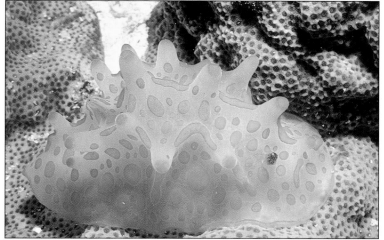

Left Soft, little polyps built the rocklike cups that form this turret coral. Each polyp is like a very tiny sea anemone. At night its tentacles come out of its cup to catch the tiny things it eats.

Above A sea slug on Australia's Great Barrier Reef. Some sea slugs eat seaweeds, others eat sea anemones or jellyfish. If a sea slug swallows jellyfish stings, these protect it from its enemies.

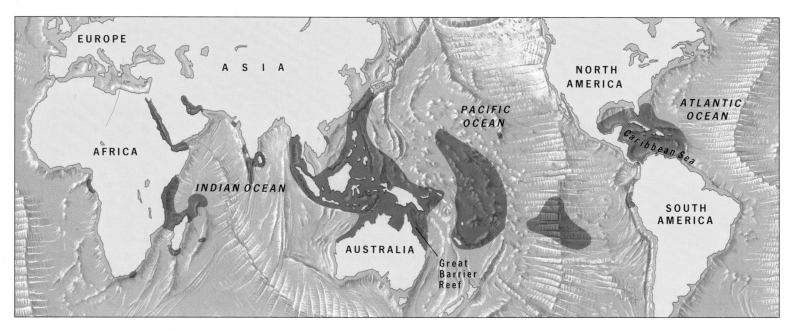

EUROPE

ASIA

AFRICA

INDIAN OCEAN

AUSTRALIA

Great Barrier Reef

PACIFIC OCEAN

NORTH AMERICA

ATLANTIC OCEAN

Caribbean Sea

SOUTH AMERICA

Above The map shows the areas where coral reefs occur. Fringing reefs are narrow reefs off coasts. Barrier reefs are offshore coral platforms. Atolls are islands shaped like necklaces.

Below The crown of thorns starfish is one of the worst enemies of corals that live in the Pacific Ocean. It crawls around on coral, feeding on the little coral polyps. Eventually, these starfish can destroy whole areas of reef.

Above Some butterfly fish have long, slim snouts. They probe for food among narrow crevices in the coral. They eat worms, tiny shellfish, and crustaceans (animals such as shrimps).

THE OPEN SEA

Just as different groups of land animals live on mountains and the plains below, so different groups of creatures live at different levels in the sea. Most stay near the surface. Deeper down it is too dark for plants to grow, and almost all sea animals depend on plants in one way or another for food.

Parts of the ocean surface are like a thin soup full of tiny drifting plants and animals, known as plankton. Many are too small for us to see without a microscope. Tiny planktonic plants form food for little planktonic animals including young fish, crabs, and jellyfish. These creatures in turn form food for larger animals.

For example, shrimplike copepods become meals for fish called herrings. Young herrings are a food for bigger fish like mackerel. Mackerel are eaten by sharks, porpoises, diving seabirds, and humans. Surprisingly, the biggest whales only eat shoals of tiny shrimplike animals.

No continents separate the oceans completely, so sea creatures could roam around the world. But many stay in just one region. Sea turtles and whale sharks (the biggest fish of all), for example, prefer waters that are always warm.

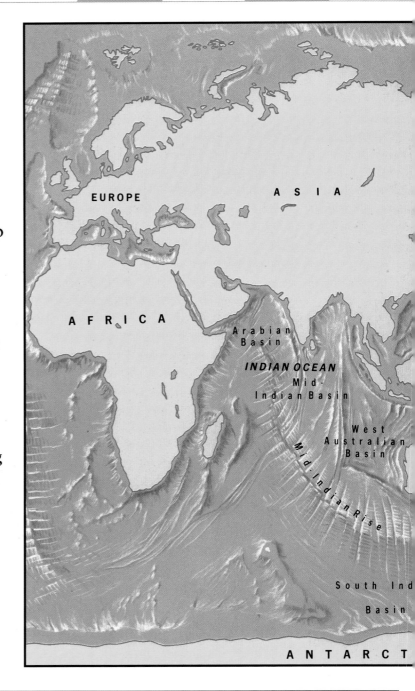

EUROPE

ASIA

AFRICA

Arabian Basin

INDIAN OCEAN
Mid-Indian Basin

West Australian Basin

Mid-Indian Rise

South Ind Basin

ANTARCT

Plankton puzzles

The young of some animals look very different from the adult versions. For instance, a very young shore crab looks rather like a mosquito larva. Later, it seems to be half crab, half lobster and only starts looking like a crab when it tucks its tail beneath its body and the body grows broader than it is long. Other oddities are the young of starfish, which are blobs of jelly, and sea squirts, which are like tadpoles.

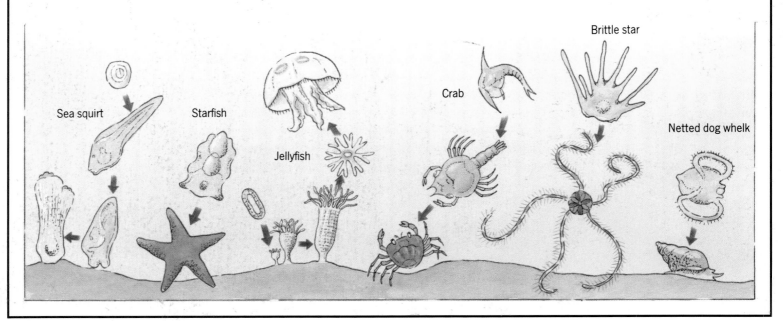

Sea squirt Starfish Jellyfish Crab Brittle star Netted dog whelk

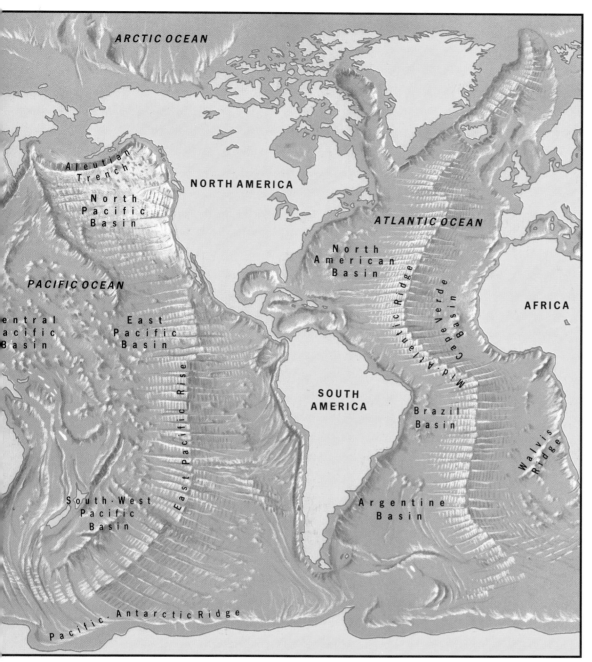

ARCTIC OCEAN

NORTH AMERICA

Aleutian Trench

North Pacific Basin

PACIFIC OCEAN

ATLANTIC OCEAN

North American Basin

AFRICA

Central Pacific Basin

East Pacific Basin

Mid-Atlantic Ridge

Cape Verde Basin

SOUTH AMERICA

East Pacific Rise

Brazil Basin

Walvis Ridge

South-West Pacific Basin

Argentine Basin

Pacific-Antarctic Ridge

Above A jellyfish drifts below the surface. Its trailing tentacles have stinging cells that the jellyfish uses to paralyze its prey.

Left The seas and oceans have a landscape as varied as the land above water. There are high mountains and great, deep trenches and vast plains of sand and mud. The seas are shallowest around the edges of the land. These areas are called the continental shelves. Currents and tides mean the oceans of the world are never still.

Below Sharks are fast, streamlined swimmers with several rows of sharp teeth for catching fish smaller than themselves. New teeth replace the old ones as they drop out. Unlike most fish, sharks have a gristly (not a bony) skeleton.

Left Green turtles swim in the world's warm inshore waters and eat sea grasses. They are large, weighing up to 830 lbs (375 kg).

Below Bottle-nosed dolphins are small whales. They are expert swimmers, who never leave the sea. They give birth to their young under water but must come to the surface for air.

THE LOWER DEPTHS

The deeper down you go into the sea, the darker and colder it becomes. By 650 feet (200 meters) down there is hardly any light. Yet deep-sea fish and other creatures live far deeper down than that.

At night, fish, squid, and prawns come up to feed upon the plankton animals. By dawn they dive down to the darker, safer depths. Many deep-sea creatures hunt one another. Others eat the dead and dying animals and plants that drift like snowflakes from the surface.

Deep-sea fish look very strange indeed. Big eyes help some tell friends from enemies in the gloom. Little lights along fishes' sides are another useful guide. Fish with huge mouths and elastic stomachs make the most of the few big meals that come their way.

Below these swimmers, other creatures feed on the scraps that settle on the ocean floor. Down here live shellfish, worms, crabs, shrimps, and sea cucumbers, long-bodied relatives of the starfish found on rocky shores.

Left Animals brought up to the sea surface often turn out to be the larvae (young) of adults that appear much more familiar to us. This decapod larva belongs to the group of crustaceans including crabs, lobsters, and shrimps.

Below This deep-sea angler fish was caught off northwest Africa. The glowing light above its head lures tiny fish within reach of its huge jaws armed with long, sharp teeth.

Deep-sea dwellers

A cross section through an ocean shows some of the creatures that live at different levels in the sea. Small drifting creatures such as jellyfish and sea gooseberries share the sunlit upper levels with fish such as sailfish, sharks, and sunfish. Even the bottom-dwelling plaice and octopus may live in shallow inshore waters. Squid and certain other creatures swim up at night and down again by day. But most creatures shown here in the lowest levels always live deep down where the only lights are given off by many of the animals themselves. Three long fins that serve as props let the tripod fish rest on a soft muddy ocean floor without sinking into the mud.

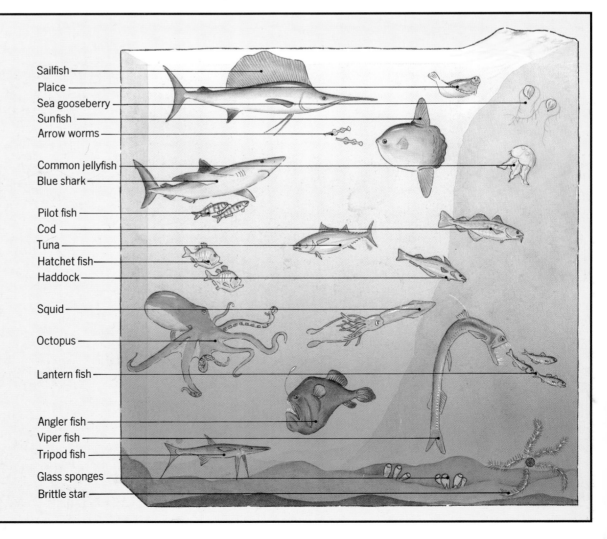

Sailfish
Plaice
Sea gooseberry
Sunfish
Arrow worms
Common jellyfish
Blue shark
Pilot fish
Cod
Tuna
Hatchet fish
Haddock
Squid
Octopus
Lantern fish
Angler fish
Viper fish
Tripod fish
Glass sponges
Brittle star

Below A chunk cut across an ocean and its floor might look like this. Creatures live at every level, even at the bottom of ocean trenches deep enough to drown the highest mountain on Earth.

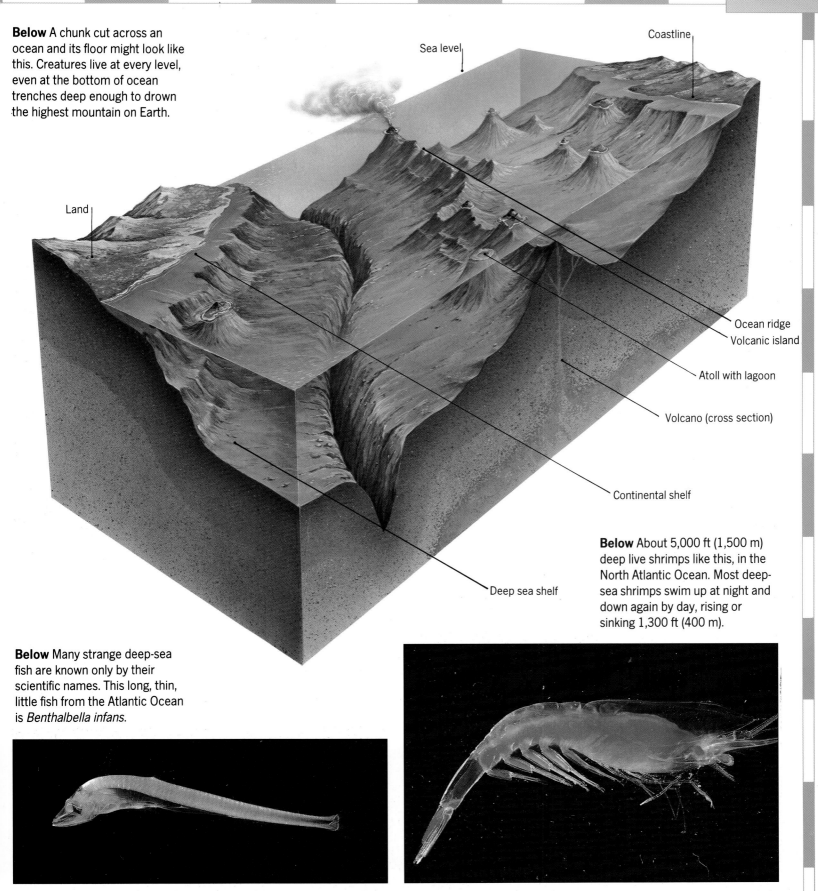

Sea level

Coastline

Land

Ocean ridge

Volcanic island

Atoll with lagoon

Volcano (cross section)

Continental shelf

Deep sea shelf

Below About 5,000 ft (1,500 m) deep live shrimps like this, in the North Atlantic Ocean. Most deep-sea shrimps swim up at night and down again by day, rising or sinking 1,300 ft (400 m).

Below Many strange deep-sea fish are known only by their scientific names. This long, thin, little fish from the Atlantic Ocean is *Benthalbella infans*.

Luminous fish

Seen from below, a hatchet fish glows. Rows of bluish lights shine from low down on each side of its body. Hatchet fish also have big, upward-facing eyes. With these they see and recognize other hatchet fish nearby by the special pattern of their lights.

Hatchet fish are silvery little creatures no longer than a finger. Despite their relatively small size they have enormous, powerful jaws and are ferocious hunters. Their curved eyes, which see in most directions, are always on the lookout for food.

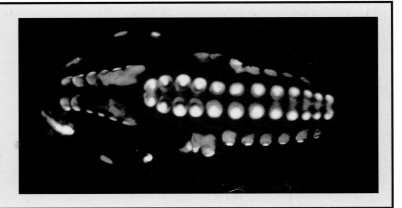

FROZEN OCEANS

Thick ice lies like a lid on the Arctic Ocean around the North Pole and around Antarctica in the south. Sea ice covers even more of these cold polar waters in winter.

All polar creatures can stand the intense cold. Birds and mammals have thick fat, fur, or feathers to keep in their body heat. Some fish even have a kind of natural antifreeze in their blood. Tiny shrimplike animals called krill teem in Antarctic waters. They would die if the water warmed much above freezing. In both polar regions, krill or similar creatures are food for fish, squid, seals, seabirds, and the largest of the whales.

In the Arctic Ocean, cracks in the ice are homes to polar cod, which hide there from seabirds, ringed seals, white whales, and narwhals. Polar bears swim out to the sea ice to hunt ringed seals.

Most penguins live in Antarctic waters. These tubby birds waddle awkwardly on land. Their wings are flippers – useless for flying but just right for swimming fast and steering through the water to catch fish. Emperor penguins also hunt squid, and Adélie penguins and crab-eater seals feast on shoals of krill.

Swimming penguins must watch out for hungry leopard seals and killer whales. On the shore, many penguin eggs and chicks fall prey to seabirds.

Above Gigantic slabs of ice jostle in the sea just off Antarctica. In winter, the slabs stick together and the sea is hidden beneath a solid sheet of ice.

Below Rival elephant seal bulls threaten one another. These are the largest of all seals. They come ashore to mate and breed on the islands around Antarctica.

Killer whales and their prey

A killer whale (left) peers above the surface of the sea, perhaps looking for prey such as the Adélie penguins (right). The huge black-and-white killer whales usually hunt in packs. They will attack penguins, seals, and small whales. Camera crews have filmed killer whales rushing up from the sea to seize young sea lions resting on a beach. In fact, their main food is fish and squid.

Penguins, like the Adélies above, have every reason to fear the killer whale, as well as their other enemy, the fierce leopard seal. All of the 18 kinds of penguins in the world live south of the equator, feeding in the food-rich waters that flow around or from Antarctica. In the sea their white bellies and dark backs blend with their background, hiding them from enemies above or below.

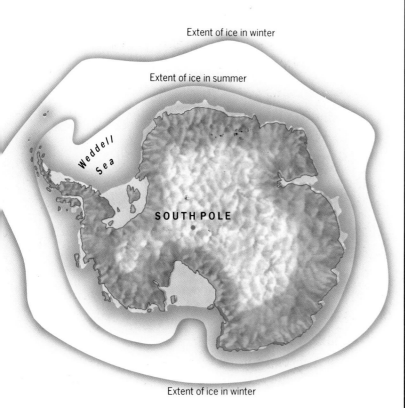

Extent of ice in winter

Extent of ice in summer

Weddell Sea

SOUTH POLE

Extent of ice in winter

Above An ice sheet thousands of feet thick sits upon Antarctica, and in places huge ice shelves jut out from the land. All this frozen water chills the oceans around Antarctica. Large stretches of sea near the land stay frozen all year. In winter, ice creeps even farther out. In summer, this sea ice breaks up into floes – drifting

KEY

 Land uncovered in summer

slabs that spread out until they cover more than 17 percent of the world's oceans. The floes slowly melt and vanish as they head north into warmer waters.

The Arctic Ocean

The Arctic is an ice-covered ocean surrounded by land. The northern edges of Europe, Asia, and North America all border the Arctic Ocean. The sea around the North Pole is permanently frozen, and in the winter the ice spreads farther across the ocean. Polar bears are the largest land animals living in the Arctic. They roam across huge areas — traveling both on the land around the Arctic Ocean and across the ice that covers it.

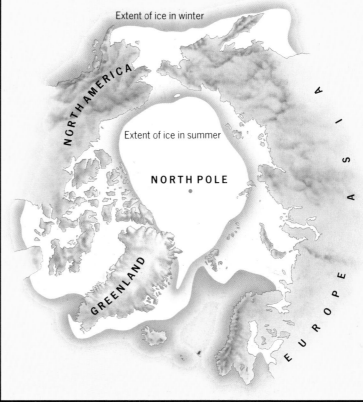

Extent of ice in winter

NORTH AMERICA

Extent of ice in summer

NORTH POLE

ASIA

GREENLAND

EUROPE

Tusks as tools

Arctic waters are the home of walruses, the big seal-like animals with two long tusks that jut down from the upper jaw. A walrus can use its massive tusks in several ways. They can be weapons to threaten rival males or their enemies, the polar bears. They also serve as rakes to loosen shellfish from the seabed so the walrus can eat them. They even act as grappling hooks to help a walrus haul its heavy body from the sea onto a floating slab of ice. Indeed the walrus's scientific name *Odobenus* means "tooth walker."

Above Emperor penguins slide or waddle over ice to reach their Antarctic breeding grounds. In midwinter each female lays an egg. A male keeps this warm while the female returns to the sea to feed. Two months later she brings back food for the chick.

Some animals make regular journeys, traveling from one place to another and back again, often in the course of a year. Such journeys are called migrations. These migrations are made as the animals search for the best places for finding food and rearing young.

TRAVEL BY AIR

Birds are among the champion long-distance migrants. In the fall, millions of warblers, waterfowl, birds of prey, and others leave northern North America, Europe, and Asia. Crossing mountains, seas, and deserts, they fly south to escape the winter cold. Some journey thousands of miles. In spring they fly back north to lay their eggs and raise their young, for there is plenty to eat in the north's long summer days.

Before setting off, migrating birds eat well and fatten up. Fat can make up half their body weight and gives them the energy to fly for days without a meal. Most migrants follow the same routes, called flyways. Some birds fly as high as 20,000 feet (6,000 meters).

Scientists have long puzzled about how birds find their way on these long journeys. They now think they use the sun and stars as a guide and may have a kind of natural compass in their brains that helps to keep them heading in the right direction.

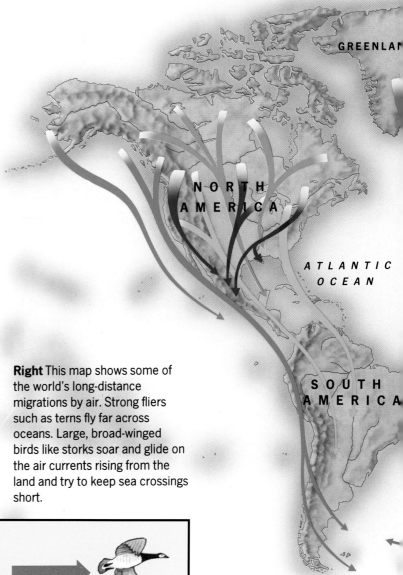

Right This map shows some of the world's long-distance migrations by air. Strong fliers such as terns fly far across oceans. Large, broad-winged birds like storks soar and glide on the air currents rising from the land and try to keep sea crossings short.

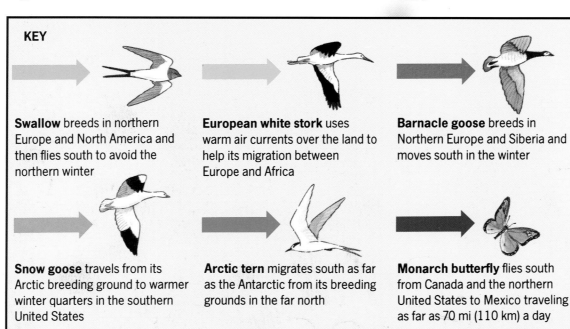

KEY

Swallow breeds in northern Europe and North America and then flies south to avoid the northern winter

European white stork uses warm air currents over the land to help its migration between Europe and Africa

Barnacle goose breeds in Northern Europe and Siberia and moves south in the winter

Snow goose travels from its Arctic breeding ground to warmer winter quarters in the southern United States

Arctic tern migrates south as far as the Antarctic from its breeding grounds in the far north

Monarch butterfly flies south from Canada and the northern United States to Mexico traveling as far as 70 mi (110 km) a day

Right The Arctic tern makes the longest migratory journey of all. It travels distances of 12,000 mi (20,000 km) from its breeding grounds in the Arctic to the Antarctic to avoid the winter cold and darkness of the far north.

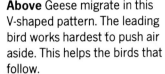

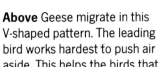

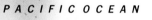

Above Geese migrate in this V-shaped pattern. The leading bird works hardest to push air aside. This helps the birds that follow.

Butterfly travelers

Birds are not the only flying migrants. Monarch butterflies fly south from as far north as Canada to winter in Mexico. The next year they fly back north. On the way they breed and die, but their young fly on.

A R C T I C

A R C T I C   O C E A N

E U R O P E

S I B E R I A

A S I A

A F R I C A

P A C I F I C   O C E A N

I N D I A N   O C E A N

A U S T R A L I A

A N T A R C T I C

Below Swallows resting on a ship during their long migration. North American swallows fly to South America for the winter, while European swallows travel to Africa.

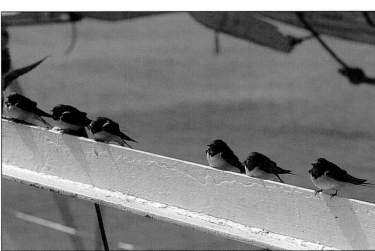

TRAVELS OVERLAND

No land animals migrate as far as many birds, but as the seasons change some big plant-eating mammals make journeys overland.

As summer fades in North America, mule deer move down mountain slopes to warmer places. Herds of caribou leave the open tundra of the far north and trudge south for hundreds of miles to spend the winter in the shelter of the northern forests. The following spring they march back north to breed, and the deer move back up the mountains.

Meanwhile, saiga antelopes living on the steppes of Asia head south to escape the worst winter cold. In spring they wander north again to eat the fresh green shoots that sprout there.

Some insects seem almost always on the move. From their loose, white, tent-shaped web, North American tent caterpillars roam to and fro in search of leaves to eat. Tropical army ants have no fixed home. Up to half a million march through the forest eating any small creature in their path. From time to time they clump together while their queen lays up to 300,000 eggs. When these hatch, the army column marches off again, carrying its young.

Below Land migrations are never as long as those by sea or air, but they happen for the same sorts of reasons: the search for food and good breeding areas. This map shows the routes of some long overland migrations.

Left A herd of wildebeest making their way across the Serengeti National Park, in East Africa. In the wet season these big antelopes graze in the southeast of the park. As the grass dries up, they move west where heavier rain has helped the grass grow more strongly. Later they will move on again to find fresh pastures to the north.

EUROPE

Steppes

ASIA

AFRICA

INDIAN OCEAN

Army ants

A column of African army ants crosses a bare patch of ground. Animals in their path would be wise to get out of their way. The workers and huge-jawed soldiers quickly rid any house of rats and mice. It is even said the ants can kill a tethered horse.

Above Caribou migrate across a frozen inlet in the Canadian Arctic. They must move far to find winter shelter. Their pale coats help to hide them from wolves.

Right Polar bears roam far over snow and ice in search of food and a mate. Hunting bears may swim across stretches of sea and drift long distances on ice floes.

A R C T I C   O C E A N

N O R T H A M E R I C A

P A C I F I C   O C E A N

A T L A N T I C   O C E A N

U S T R A L I A

KEY

Caribou, or reindeer, move south to avoid the bitter cold of the arctic winter

Polar bear roams great distances over land and icy frozen ocean

Wildebeest, or gnu, migrate during the dry season to find new grazing areas

Saiga antelope, once in danger of extinction, moves south in winter

SEA JOURNEYS

At night squid rise hundreds of feet to the sea surface to feed. By dawn they dive back down into the safe dark depths. In the fall, off the Bahama Islands, rows of spiny lobsters march across the ocean floor to deep water undisturbed by storms.

These are just short trips. Some fish and sea mammals make far longer underwater journeys. Tuna fish that spawn in the Mediterranean Sea may swim north as far as Scandinavia to find food. Whales travel thousands of miles between their feeding grounds in the far north or south and the warm waters where they give birth to their young. Sea turtles also make long trips back to their breeding grounds. Green turtles that feed off the Atlantic coast of South America swim over 600 miles (1,000 kilometers) to lay their eggs on tiny Ascension Island. The smell and taste of ocean currents help them find their way.

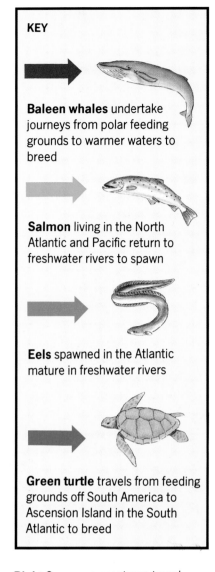

KEY

Baleen whales undertake journeys from polar feeding grounds to warmer waters to breed

Salmon living in the North Atlantic and Pacific return to freshwater rivers to spawn

Eels spawned in the Atlantic mature in freshwater rivers

Green turtle travels from feeding grounds off South America to Ascension Island in the South Atlantic to breed

Right Some sea creatures travel huge distances to reach freshwater breeding grounds or to find fresh supplies of food

Below Sockeye salmon leap to clear a waterfall. After years at sea they have swum back into the river where they hatched. Upstream they will spawn.

Once in a lifetime

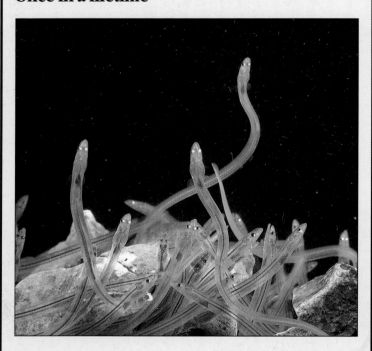

Some underwater journeys happen only once in a lifetime. European and American eels spawn in the southern North Atlantic and leave the tiny eel larvae to drift with the currents. The American larvae take about a year to reach the east coast of the United States. European larvae may take three years to reach coastal waters. The larvae become thin, transparent elvers (above) and swim up freshwater rivers. Here they take up to 12 years to mature before beginning their long journey back to the spawning grounds. Having spawned, they probably die.

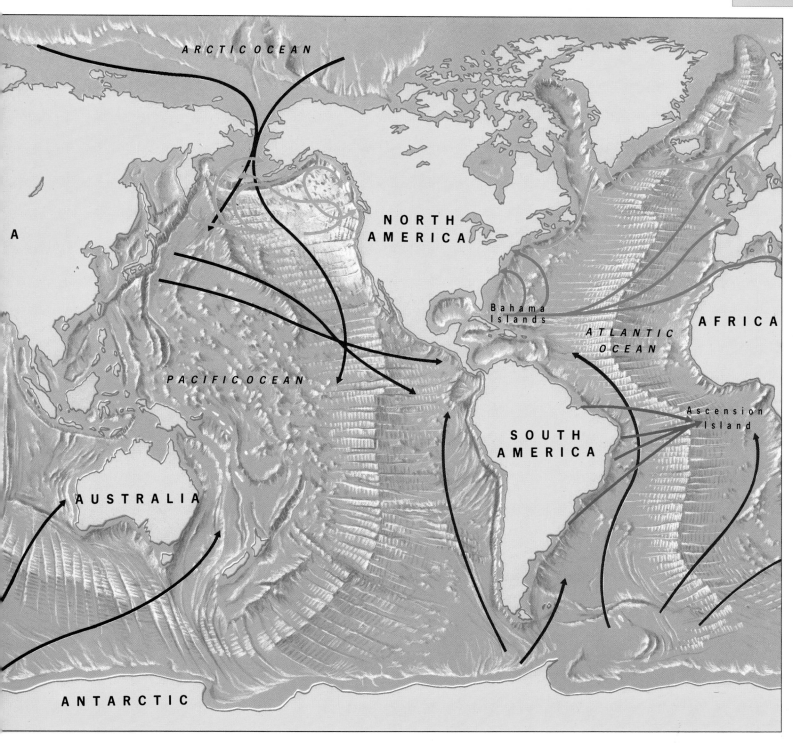

ARCTIC OCEAN

NORTH
AMERICA

A

PACIFIC OCEAN

Bahama
Islands

ATLANTIC
OCEAN

AFRICA

AUSTRALIA

SOUTH
AMERICA

Ascension
Island

ANTARCTIC

Whales

The gray whale (left) and blue whale (below) both make long sea migrations twice a year. Gray whales swim inshore as they migrate up and down the North Pacific Ocean. Blue whales are much rarer and swim in deeper water far from land. Few people ever get a glimpse of them.

EARLY LIFE – IN WATER AND ON LAND

The earliest life-forms – simple, single-celled living things – gradually evolved. From these, a variety of plants and animals developed. By 680 million years ago, worms, jellyfish, and other soft-bodied creatures crawled or floated in a sea in what is now Australia. By 550 million years ago, a strange little leaf-shaped creature had evolved with a stiffening rod in its back – it was the first animal with something like a backbone. Creatures like that gave rise to the first fishes. As these evolved, so too did sea creatures such as trilobites (somewhat like woodlice) and giant sea scorpions.

There could be no animals on land until there were land plants – for all animals depend on plants for food. Plants began to grow on land about 450 million years ago. The first animals to follow them were small invertebrates, such as worms. By 410 million years ago, early relatives of centipedes, scorpions, and spiders scuttled over what is now Europe and the United States.

Such creatures became food for backboned land animals. The first of these – the lobe-finned fishes – eventually gave rise to amphibians, which were the earliest backboned animals with legs. Their descendants were the reptiles, which had much tougher skins and laid waterproof eggs. These made it possible for them to leave moist, watery places and spread into dry uplands.

Left Trilobites are now extinct, but between 600 and 250 million years ago they swam and crawled below the sea. These were among the first animals with well-developed eyes. They looked a bit like woodlice do today. This is a fossil – the remains of a trilobite preserved in rock.

The story of Earth

Our planet formed about 4.6 billion years ago. At first, there was no water, or air fit to breathe. Volcanoes erupted on the Earth's surface. Then the surface cooled, and continents and oceans formed.

The first living things – tiny bacteria and algae – appeared in the sea about a billion years later. It took another 3 billion years for life to spread onto the land.

First land plants   First amphibians
500 million years ago
← Reign of dinosaurs →
Now
● First seaweeds and jellyfish
1.6 billion years ago
● First green algae
First blue-green algae produce oxygen
2.8 billion years ago
4 billion years ago
● First algae
4.6 billion years ago

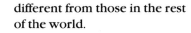

Drifting continents

The Earth's surface has not always looked like it does today. All the land was joined together at one time. About 200 million years ago the landmass began to split up. The shape of today's continents began to emerge about 100 million years ago. Australia became separated from Europe, Asia, and Africa very early on. This is why the mammals there are very different from those in the rest of the world.

280 million years ago   200 million years ago   100 million years ago   5 million years ago

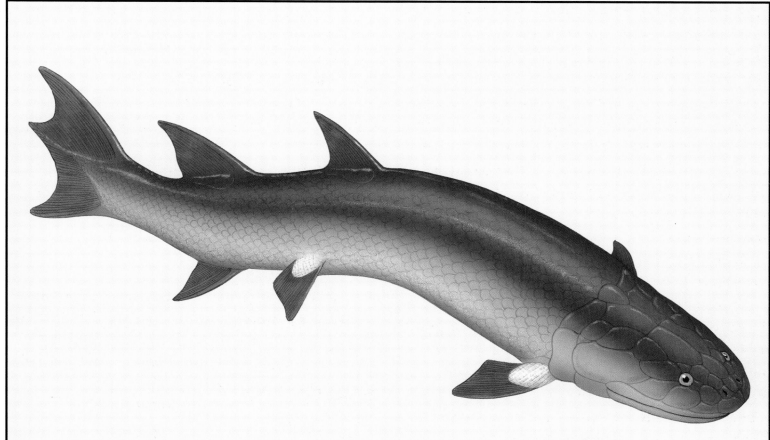

Above *Eusthenopteron* was an unusual flesh-eating freshwater fish that grew up to 24 in (60 cm) long. It lived about 370 million years ago in what are now North America and Europe. It had lungs so it could breathe air at the surface if hot weather turned the water foul. This fish also had strong, stubby fins. A baby *Eusthenopteron* could have skipped ashore to escape a big hungry adult. It might have stayed on land to snap up little creepy-crawly creatures.

Fin to foot

From lobe-finned fish like *Eusthenopteron* came amphibians and reptiles: four-legged animals that walked on land. This came about in North America and Europe through gradual changes in the fishes' limbs. Bit by bit the pectoral (front) fins became forelimbs with fingers. The pelvic (back) fins became hind limbs with toes. Meanwhile, the bones inside these limbs grew longer and stronger to support the animals' weight.

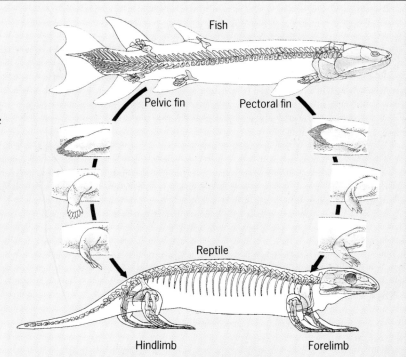

Fish

Pelvic fin   Pectoral fin

Reptile

Hindlimb   Forelimb

FROM DESERTS TO DINOSAURS

About 300 million years ago, when all the continents were still one mass of land, little rain fell inland. The world was largely desert. Long-tailed prehistoric reptiles roamed this harsh, dry landscape.

Big sprawling mammal-like reptiles called pelycosaurs lived where the southern United States is today. Later, more advanced mammal-like reptiles called therapsids lived in places as far apart as Asia and Antarctica. *Probelesodon*, from South America, had a hairy body and must have been warm-blooded, like a mammal. By about 200 million years ago small therapsid reptiles gave rise to the first shrew-like mammals.

About 230 million years ago, there appeared a brand new group of reptiles: dinosaurs. Instead of sprawling like lizards, they walked and ran with legs below the body. The early, dog-sized dinosaurs gave rise to giants such as the huge herbivores *Brachiosaurus* and *Apatosaurus* and the carnivorous *Tyrannosaurus rex*.

For 150 million years dinosaurs were rulers of the land. As the Age of Dinosaurs wore on, continents drifted apart. New oceans stopped dinosaurs from spreading. This meant, for example, that North America's horned dinosaurs and some other groups never reached Australia.

Now, too, shallow seas invaded low-lying land. Here swam those big prehistoric reptiles the fishlike ichthyosaurs and barrel-bodied plesiosaurs. Above them flew the dinosaurs' close relatives, the skin-winged pterosaurs, and birds, descended from the dinosaurs.

From reptile to mammal

Reptiles, like the pelycosaur called *Dimetrodon*, were better adapted to life on land than the amphibians. They had stronger teeth, more efficient legs, and waterproof skins and laid eggs with a shell – so they didn't need water except to drink. Very gradually some reptiles acquired mammal-like features. Therapsid reptiles, like *Probelesodon*, looked very much like mammals do today. They had hair and were warm-blooded. *Megazostrodon* was a shrew-sized mammal that came out at night to feed on insects.

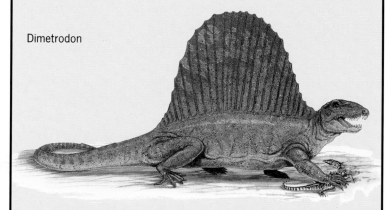

Dimetrodon

Probelesodon

Megazostrodon

Early fliers

The first flying vertebrates were reptiles called pterosaurs. These had wings formed from skin stretched over elongated "fingers." *Dimorphodon* was an early pterosaur with a big beak.

The first known bird lived about 150 million years ago. *Archaeopteryx* ("ancient wing") had feathered wings.

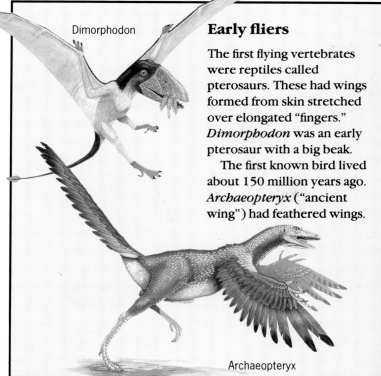

Dimorphodon

Archaeopteryx

KEY

1 Dicraeosaurus
2 Barosaurus
3 Brachiosaurus
4 Kentrosaurus

5 Dryosaurus
6 Elaphrosaurus

Below Dinosaur sizes compared with each other and with people.

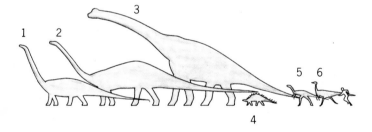

Above This scene shows what life in East Africa might have looked like about 150 million years ago during the Age of the Dinosaurs. All the dinosaurs shown were plant eaters except *Elaphrosaurus* (6), which was smaller, speedier, and possibly carnivorous.

The herbivorous dinosaurs shown all lived peacefully together browsing on plants. Their different sizes meant they fed on different plants and so were not in competition with each other.

The scene also shows some other animals that lived at the time – tiny ratlike mammals, freshwater turtles, and pigeon-sized pterosaurs with long tails and pointed teeth used for catching fish.

Below The dinosaur *Tyrannosaurus rex* was, as far as we know, the biggest meat-eating land animal ever. Up to 50 ft (15 m) long, and 20 ft (6 m) tall, it weighed more than an elephant. Although many films and books have shown it as a fierce and successful hunter, its weight would probably have prevented it from running very fast.

Tyrannosaurus rex

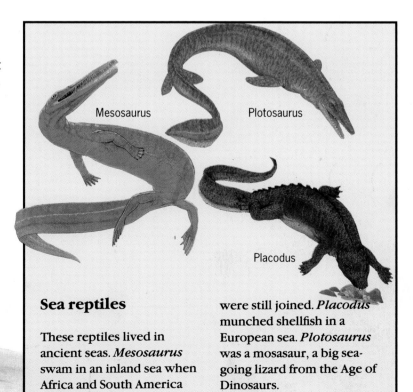

Mesosaurus

Plotosaurus

Placodus

Sea reptiles

These reptiles lived in ancient seas. *Mesosaurus* swam in an inland sea when Africa and South America were still joined. *Placodus* munched shellfish in a European sea. *Plotosaurus* was a mosasaur, a big sea-going lizard from the Age of Dinosaurs.

THE AGE OF MAMMALS

No one is quite sure why, but all the dinosaurs and most other prehistoric reptiles died out about 65 million years ago. Once the dinosaurs had gone, there were no large animals to keep the mammals in check. Small, timid, early mammals gave rise to bigger, bolder kinds. The largest lived on northern continents.

All mammals have certain things in common. They all have hair even if it is only a few tufts. Most baby mammals grow in the mother's body and are born alive. Only a few Australian mammals like the platypus and echidna lay eggs.

They all feed their young on milk produced in the mother's body, and they are all warm-blooded – they can produce heat to maintain a constant body temperature. Only mammals and birds are warm-blooded and can do this. These features have enabled mammals to live in many different climates and conditions.

By 26 million years ago, grasses were replacing trees in great tracts of North America and Asia as these areas grew cooler and drier than before. Herds of strange hoofed grazing mammals roamed the grasslands of North America. These animals had their enemies. The fiercest predators were prehistoric cats.

Above Small, early mammals lived at the same time as the large, fierce dinosaurs – but managed to survive and, in the end, outlast them. The mammals shown here were smaller than a human foot.

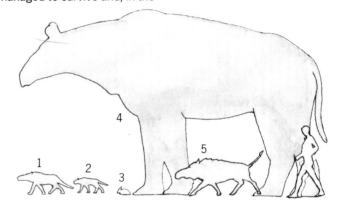

KEY

1 Hyaenodon
2 Nimravus
3 Ordolagus
4 Indricotherium
5 Entelodon

Below The mammals shown below lived about 30 million years ago in Asia. *Hyaenodon* (1) and the cat *Nimravus* (2) were meat eaters. The rabbit *Ordolagus* (3) and the giant rhinoceros *Indricotherium* (4) ate plants. The pig *Entelodon* (5) was 6 ft (2 m) long and ate almost anything.

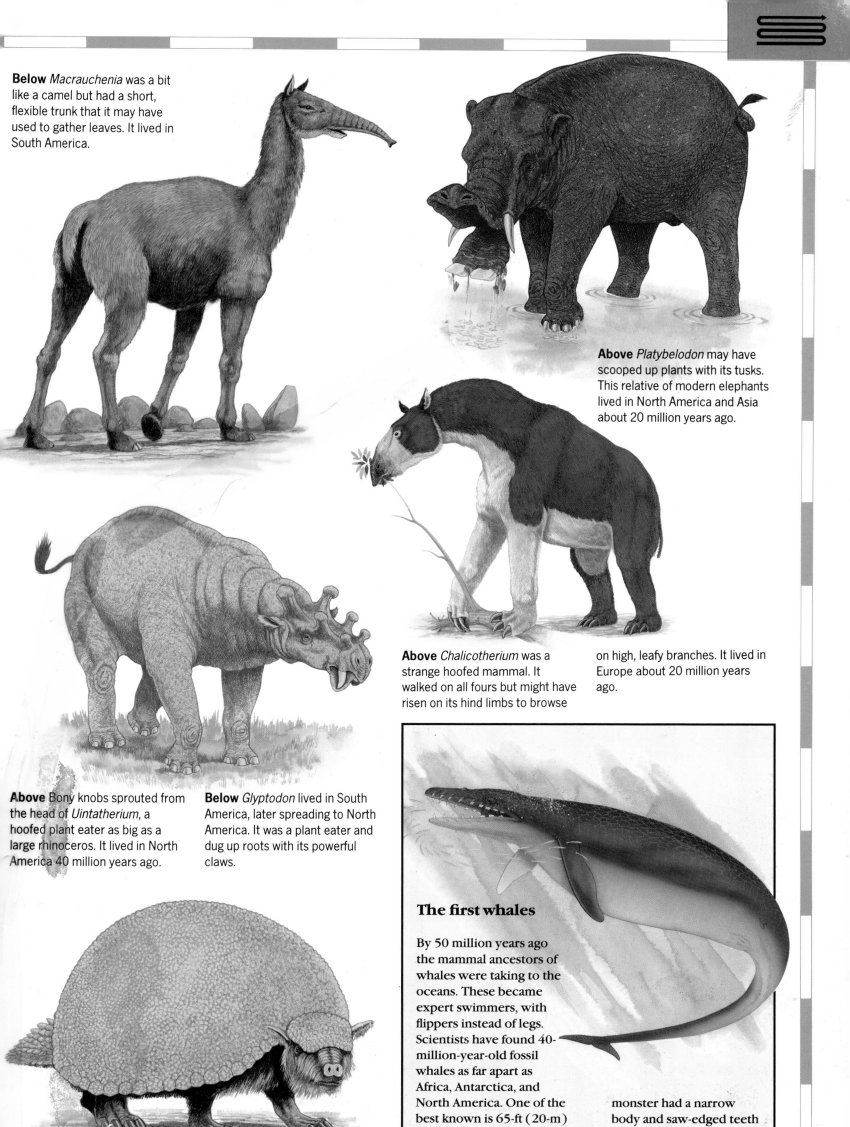

Below *Macrauchenia* was a bit like a camel but had a short, flexible trunk that it may have used to gather leaves. It lived in South America.

Above *Platybelodon* may have scooped up plants with its tusks. This relative of modern elephants lived in North America and Asia about 20 million years ago.

Above *Chalicotherium* was a strange hoofed mammal. It walked on all fours but might have risen on its hind limbs to browse on high, leafy branches. It lived in Europe about 20 million years ago.

Above Bony knobs sprouted from the head of *Uintatherium*, a hoofed plant eater as big as a large rhinoceros. It lived in North America 40 million years ago.

Below *Glyptodon* lived in South America, later spreading to North America. It was a plant eater and dug up roots with its powerful claws.

The first whales

By 50 million years ago the mammal ancestors of whales were taking to the oceans. These became expert swimmers, with flippers instead of legs. Scientists have found 40-million-year-old fossil whales as far apart as Africa, Antarctica, and North America. One of the best known is 65-ft (20-m) long *Basilosaurus*. This monster had a narrow body and saw-edged teeth for seizing fish.

ICE AGE ANIMALS

Two million years ago, an Ice Age came to all northern lands. Sheets of ice hundreds of feet thick spread over much of North America, Europe, and Asia. After thousands of years, the weather grew warmer and the ice sheets shrank. Then they spread again. This happened many times.

Hardy mammals grew hair and fur to protect them from cold. Long hairy coats covered the woolly rhinoceros and woolly mammoth (a prehistoric elephant). Both roamed chilly northern plains. Here, too, lived the shaggy-coated musk-oxen and the caribou, or reindeer. In cold forests, shaggy-coated cave bears sheltered in rocky caves.

In cold periods, advancing ice sheets forced such creatures south as far as southern Europe. When the weather warmed up, the big mammals moved back north again. As the weather warmed, not all small mammals who were adapted to the cold moved north. Some climbed high mountains instead. In this way, mountain hares now living on the European Alps got separated from their relatives, the arctic hares of the far north.

While cold-loving animals were moving north, warmth-loving animals came up from the south to take their place. About 100,000 years ago, hippopotamuses and elephants from Africa roamed beside the Thames river where London, England, stands today. When it grew chilly once again, these creatures moved south again, and woolly mammoths took their place.

Above Reindeer, brought in from Scandinavia, in the north of Britain. In Ice Age times reindeer roamed in southern Europe.

Below This map shows the farthest the north polar ice stretched in the Ice Age. It covered where New York stands today.

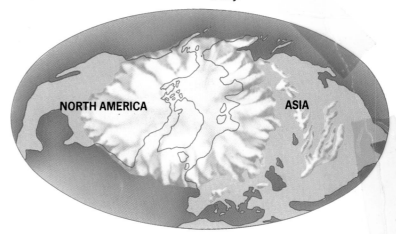

NORTH AMERICA   ASIA

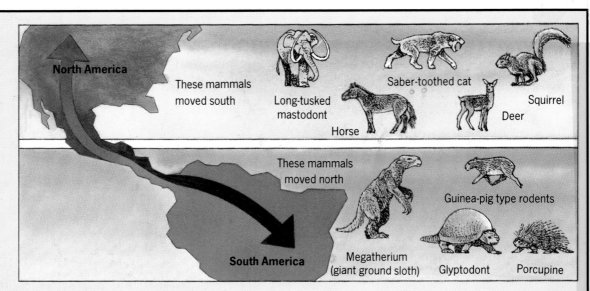

North and South America

By Ice Age times, a land bridge had risen to join North and South America, and animals could cross between them. Animals from the north moved south, and some animals from the south moved north. Some animals became extinct because, where they met, similar animals competed for food.

North America

These mammals moved south

Long-tusked mastodont

Saber-toothed cat

Squirrel

Deer

Horse

These mammals moved north

Guinea-pig type rodents

South America

Megatherium (giant ground sloth)

Glyptodont

Porcupine

Below These creatures coped with cold in Ice Age Europe, 40,000 years ago. Some kinds are still alive today. The Arctic hare (1), musk-ox (2), and reindeer (3) are plant eaters of the far northern tundra. The northern lynx (7) still hunts in northern forests. The wolf (4) prowls after reindeer and musk-oxen. Crows (10) still search for dead animals to eat. The other Ice Age creatures shown are all extinct.

KEY

1 Arctic hare
2 Musk-oxen
3 Reindeer
4 Wolf
5 Cave bear
6 Mammoth
7 Lynx
8 Woolly rhinoceros
9 Giant deer
10 Crow
11 Neanderthal man

Different cats

Two unrelated kinds of flesh-eating mammals evolved amazingly long, stabbing upper teeth. *Thylacosmilus* was a marsupial 'cat' that lived in South America. Its two upper canine teeth grew like long daggers or the curved swords called sabers. When its mouth was shut, both teeth fitted into skin sheaths in its lower jaw. *Smilodon* was a true cat that lived in North and South America rather later. It also had saberlike canine teeth. Both saber-tooth cats had very strong neck muscles to pull the head sharply down and drive its fangs into the prey.

Thylacosmilus (marsupial saber-toothed cat)

Smilodon (placental saber-toothed cat)

Thylacosmilus

THE FIRST PEOPLE

Today, most animals are at the mercy of just one kind of animal – ourselves. Unlike most animals, people can build their homes in many different kinds of habitats. Our big, thinking brains and nimble fingers have helped us to change the world to suit ourselves. The changes we have made are huge. Forests have been cut down, wetlands have been drained, and cities have been built on once fertile land.

The first people were gatherers of any wild foods they could find. They lived in warm, dry parts of Africa, and their ancestors were apes.

Some five million years ago a prehistoric African ape gave rise to more human-looking creatures. They were like large chimpanzees. But they walked upright, which freed their hands to make simple tools.

These man-apes roamed the dry open grasslands that were replacing forests in East Africa. Big, meaty grazing animals lived here, too. So did leopards, lions, and hyenas. Two million years ago, a man-ape gave rise to a creature skilled at stealing meat from the animals these carnivores had killed. This was

Human ancestors

The pictures below show three human ancestors:
1. *Homo habilis* – "handy man"
2. *Homo erectus* – "upright man"
3. Neanderthal man – who lived about 230,000 to 30,000 years ago
These early "humans" gave rise to modern people.

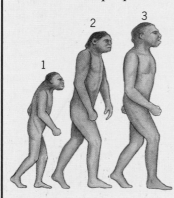

Left Many early people who lived by hunting and gathering wild plants created paintings. This picture of animals was made by the Anasazi people in North America about a thousand years ago.

Right The remains of the village of Skara Brae in Orkney, Scotland, in northern Europe. People lived here about 4,500 years ago. They had stone "furniture." You can see the shelves on the far wall, the beds on the right and left, and a hearth in the center.

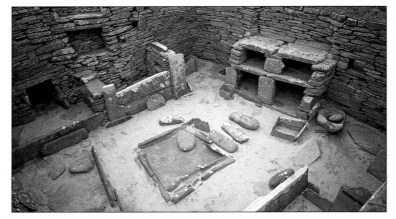

Right Modern humans are varied in appearance. Their differences in skin color developed in the distant past, in different parts of the world, and were often related to the climate people lived in.

the first known human: "handy man".

By one and a half million years ago, little handy man had probably given rise to a taller, bigger-brained upright human. This creature spread beyond Africa.

The first modern people probably appeared in Africa 200,000 years ago. They were hunter-gatherers who could speak, keep warm with fire and clothing, and hunt with finely pointed weapons. By 30,000 years ago, such people had reached all the continents of the world except Antarctica.

Versatile people

People can live in lots of different places. In cold lands we wear warm clothes. In hot deserts we can protect ourselves from the sun and use desert creatures, like the camel, to carry us. We have discovered how to fly and how to travel underwater. Our skills have changed and destroyed many habitats.

Above In cold lands people may wear clothes made from the warm coats of animals.

Above People cannot fly like birds, but we can build airplanes to carry us.

Below People cannot swim like fish, but we can travel on land and in water.

Below Most animals that live in cold lands could not adapt to life in the dry desert, but people can.

DOMESTICATED ANIMALS

More than 10,000 years ago, people in southwest Asia began keeping animals and planting crops to eat. Cultivated plants and tame animals supplied more food than people could get by hunting wild animals and gathering wild plants. More food meant fewer people starved, so human beings multiplied and did not have to spend all their time finding food.

The first tame animals were most likely to have been dogs, descended from wolves. Dogs helped hunters catch and kill wild sheep and cattle. Later, hunters learned to tame and keep some cattle, sheep, and goats for meat, milk, wool, and hides. Later still, people trained camels, donkeys, horses, and llamas to pull or carry loads.

People bred only from the tamest animals and the best milk, meat, or wool producers. So domesticated animals became heavier, less agile, and less fierce than their wild relations. But they mostly still look similar.

As people moved to new lands, they took tame creatures with them. Now farms and ranches as far apart as South America, Australia, Europe, and the United States teem with sheep and cattle descended from a few wild Asian ancestors, tamed long ago.

Left Domesticated goats rest in the hot sun of a sandy semi-desert. These goats, whose floppy ears lose heat easily, have been bred for hot weather. Other goats, with thick, shaggy coats, resist the cold. Goats of various breeds are kept in almost every climate.

Below Water buffaloes help farmers work the flooded rice fields of southern and Southeast Asia. These cattle enjoy wallowing. They can plow through muddy water where other animals would get stuck.

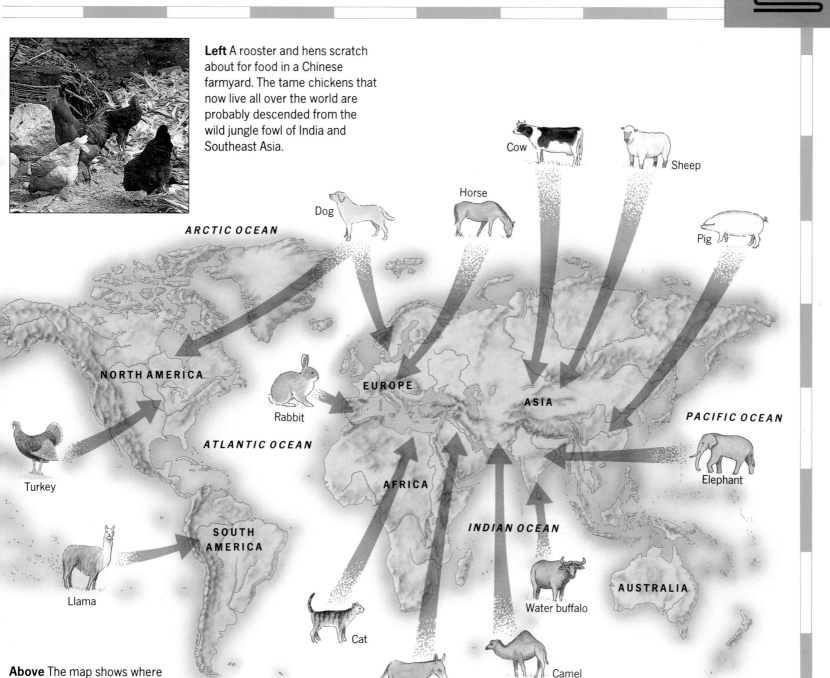

Left A rooster and hens scratch about for food in a Chinese farmyard. The tame chickens that now live all over the world are probably descended from the wild jungle fowl of India and Southeast Asia.

Above The map shows where many of the domestic animals we know today originally came from.

Altered animals

Old bones and teeth often help to show if a prehistoric animal had been domesticated.

Tame sheep have shorter legs than wild sheep, and most tame sheep have no horns. Tame pigs have shorter jaws than wild boars and lack a wild boar's tusks. Tame goats have twisted horns, but wild goats' horns are curved. The remains of cattle from the islands north of Scotland show that they had small bones. They were probably descended from dwarf forms of a wild ox.

The two pictures show the noticeable difference

between domesticated pigs (right) and the tougher, fiercer-looking wild boar (above) – almost certainly one of their ancestors.

ANIMAL INVADERS

As well as transporting domesticated breeds, people have spread wild animals around the world. For instance, in the 1800s, sportsmen took foxes and rabbits from Europe to Australia for the fun of hunting them. British settlers released blackbirds in Australia and New Zealand to remind themselves of bird song in the English countryside. Someone let loose 100 European starlings in New York City.

Meanwhile, animal stowaways on ships were landing all around the world. Black rats reached Jamaica from Europe. European house mice invaded the United States and Australia. Giant African snails were carried across the Indian and Pacific oceans. Lonely islands became new homes for animals such as mice, cats, goats, sheep, and pigs.

With no natural enemies to keep their numbers down in their new homes, invading animals could multiply unchecked. Very often, they became pests.

To limit the damage these creatures did, people shipped in the creatures' natural enemies. They thought Indian mongooses would wipe out Jamaica's black rats, European stoats would destroy rabbits in Australia, and Hawaiian giant toads would gobble up the beetles eating Australian sugar cane. But, often, further damage was done as the mongooses, stoats, and toads attacked native animals instead of the imported ones they had been brought out to destroy.

New Zealand

The photograph (below) shows a day-old red deer. This species of deer is just one of a huge number of animals that have been introduced into New Zealand since the 1830s by human settlers.

Before this New Zealand, cut off from the rest of the world at an early point, had few native animals. The animals that did live there included birds like kiwis, albatrosses, and some species of parrots, poisonous spiders, and the tuatara – a descendant of a prehistoric reptile. Besides red deer, European imports into New Zealand have included elk, chamois, goats, pigs, hares, rabbits, hedgehogs, mice, cats, and ferrets. From Australia, people brought brush-tailed possums and wallabies. Among new birds carried to New Zealand were European blackbirds, crows, geese, larks, owls, pheasants, sparrows, and starlings.

Altogether 33 kinds of mammals, 33 birds, two amphibians, a reptile, and some insects have now been introduced onto these islands. Some live harmlessly beside the native animals, but others compete with them for food.

Right Many animals have traveled with humans to new parts of the world and been able to survive if released in a similar habitat. Some have been carried to their new homes accidentally – like rats on board early sailing ships. Others have been deliberately introduced.
This map shows some animal invaders and some of the areas they have moved into.

Below Marine toads (also called giant toads or cane toads) come from South America, but farmers have let them loose on sugar plantations as far apart as Hawaii and Australia to kill beetles that eat the cane. However, they also eat many other small creatures – and poison any animals that are large enough to eat them.

Left European starlings now breed on several continents. They are seen as a pest because they foul city buildings and raid orchards.

Right Black rats from southern Asia spread far across the world on ships. Shipwrecked black and brown rats have destroyed many rare species of island animals.

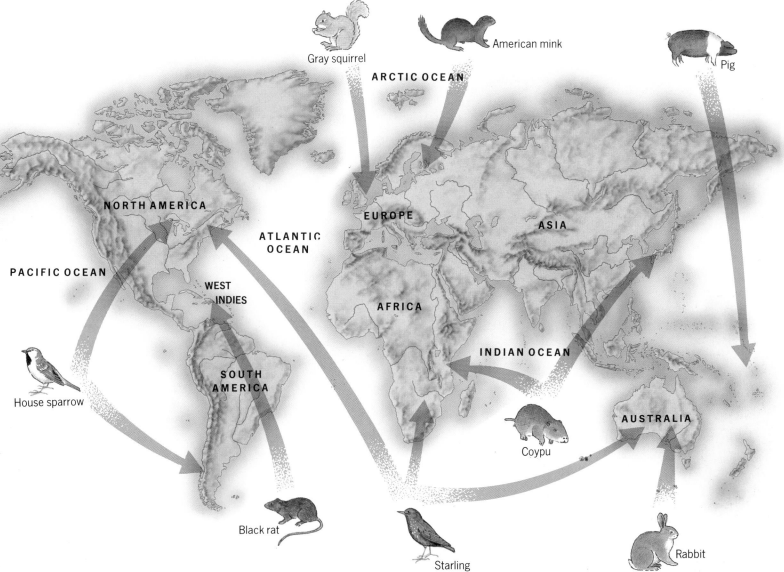

Gray squirrel

American mink

Pig

ARCTIC OCEAN

NORTH AMERICA

ATLANTIC OCEAN

PACIFIC OCEAN

EUROPE

ASIA

WEST INDIES

House sparrow

SOUTH AMERICA

AFRICA

INDIAN OCEAN

AUSTRALIA

Coypu

Black rat

Starling

Rabbit

Below This rabbit was photographed in Australia, although its ancestors came from Europe. Introduced rabbits bred quickly in Australia and are now serious pests on farms.

Right The small Indian mongoose was brought to the West Indies and Hawaii to kill rats. Sadly, the mongooses started killing off rare native animals.

VANISHING ANIMALS

Although humans have helped a few kinds of farm animals to spread and multiply, we have destroyed wild creatures by the thousands. This process probably started more than 10,000 years ago, when our ancestors hunted animals for food.

Later, farmers began to kill off big wild animals that harmed farm animals or crops. On small island communities, like Britain, several kinds have been wiped out completely. The bears, wild boar, and wolves that once roamed the country were all killed off hundreds of years ago. They survive elsewhere, but many of the world's birds and other animals are actually extinct. For instance, seamen killed off the huge arctic Steller's sea cow 200 years ago. The world's last quagga (a kind of zebra from Africa) went in 1883. The last passenger pigeon died in the United States in 1914.

Now many other animals are dying out. Poachers may destroy Africa's black rhinoceroses and mountain gorillas, but losing their homes is the main risk to most threatened animals. As people multiply, they want more land for growing food and building cities. To get this land they burn and cut down trees, plow up grasslands, and drain marshes. As these habitats disappear, so do the animals.

The great auk

Above China's giant panda is probably the most famous endangered animal. Only about 1,000 still live in the wild.

Below Rhinoceroses have become a rare sight in East Africa. Poachers have killed thousands of these creatures for their horns. In many parts of the world rhino horns are valued for their supposed magical and medicinal properties.

Long ago, North Atlantic fishermen killed and ate large numbers of a big sea bird called the great auk. The great auk swam and dived well, but it was clumsy on land and could not fly. On the rocky islands where it nested, hungry sailors could catch it easily. In 1730, there were still millions nesting in Greenland, but overhunting soon reduced these numbers. In 1840 hunters killed the last two. Now the only great auks left are stuffed like the one shown above.

Left Here, loggers have cut down and burned part of a rain forest in South America. The trees beyond remind us what the land was like before. As trees fell, forest creatures lost their homes. Monkeys, parrots, lizards, snakes, frogs, beetles, and many more were killed.

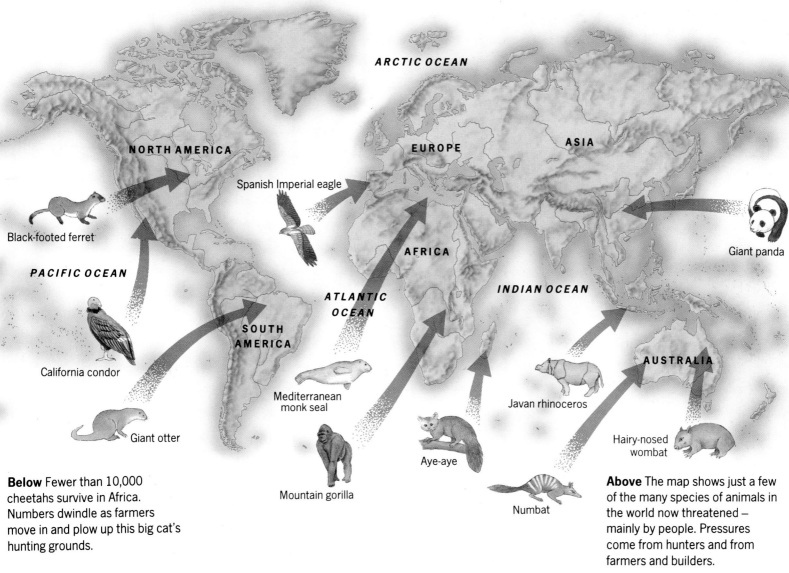

ARCTIC OCEAN

NORTH AMERICA

EUROPE

ASIA

Spanish Imperial eagle

Black-footed ferret

PACIFIC OCEAN

AFRICA

Giant panda

California condor

ATLANTIC OCEAN

SOUTH AMERICA

INDIAN OCEAN

AUSTRALIA

Mediterranean monk seal

Javan rhinoceros

Giant otter

Aye-aye

Hairy-nosed wombat

Mountain gorilla

Numbat

Below Fewer than 10,000 cheetahs survive in Africa. Numbers dwindle as farmers move in and plow up this big cat's hunting grounds.

Above The map shows just a few of the many species of animals in the world now threatened — mainly by people. Pressures come from hunters and from farmers and builders.

Right An African elephant and her calf wander through a protected national park. African elephants grew scarcer in the 1980s as poachers killed them for their ivory tusks. Traders smuggled loads of tusks to several Asian countries. Craftsmen then carved them into ivory ornaments and sold them for high prices. In many African countries, there are now strict rules against poaching ,and armed game wardens try to protect the elephants. Outside Africa new laws against buying ivory have also helped to stop the killing.

SAVING THE WORLD'S WILDLIFE

The world's wild animals are disappearing fast. What can be done to stop the most endangered creatures from dying out?

There seems little chance of saving species like the Javan rhinoceros or California condor. Very few of these are still alive. Where there are enough of a species left, captive breeding sometimes helps. Père David's deer from China and Przewalski's horse from Mongolia have both been saved this way. First, a group of these threatened animals is caught. They are allowed to breed in a zoo or an animal park. Soon there are more animals, and some are sent to other zoos or parks. If it is safe to let them go, some will be returned to the wild.

Governments protect whole groups of animals and plants by setting land aside as wildlife parks with guards to keep out herdsmen, farmers, lumberjacks, and poachers. The largest wildlife park is a forest – Canada's Wood Buffalo National Park.

The governments of many countries work together to help wildlife. They stop hunters and dealers from killing rare animals. This way, they hope to save the African elephant and the blue whale, the largest animal of all.

Much more must be done if the creatures pictured in this atlas are to survive. The world would be a duller, poorer place without them.

Above Two lesser horseshoe bats hang beside a greater horseshoe bat. In some parts of Europe, these creatures have become scarce as people have destroyed their nesting places and killed the insect pests they eat. One way of helping them is to put up bat nesting boxes.

Below Spanish Imperial eagles are among Europe's most endangered birds. Only a few dozen pairs survive, but conservation work is helping numbers to increase. There are now laws that protect them, and birds are being bred in captivity.

Left A friendly gray whale greets visitors. Once, people only thought of whales as creatures to be killed for food. Now most of us prefer to marvel at the creatures' size and intelligence. Most countries have stopped killing whales, perhaps only just in time before several species become extinct.

Right This mother and baby chimpanzee from Africa were photographed in a zoo. Breeding in captivity might be the only way to save endangered animals like these. Their homes in the wild are threatened by people who destroy habitats to establish farms.

Above Tourists photograph an unconcerned leopard. African governments need the money tourists spend, so they try hard to protect their wildlife.

Right Instead of being shot, tigers that kill farm animals can be captured and moved to protected areas.

GLOSSARY

Words in *italics* have their own entry in the glossary.

A

ALGAE kinds of water plant, without stems or leaves.

AMPHIBIAN a backboned animal, such as a frog or newt, that usually lays its eggs in water. Young amphibians usually start life in the water, with no proper limbs, and breathing through gills, like fish. As they grow older, most develop limbs and lungs and become able to live on land as well as in water.

ANIMAL a living thing that eats other living things, or their remains. Most animals can move around.

B

BACTERIA tiny one-celled living things. Many cause diseases.

BIOLOGICAL COMMUNITY a group of living things depending on each other and their surroundings for food. For example, a tree may be a biological community, with different kinds of animals feeding on the tree and each other.

BIOME also known as a life zone. A large area of land or water that suits only certain kinds of animals and plants: it may be land largely under ice and snow; cold forest; temperate forest; grassland; desert; wet, tropical rain forest; or a coral reef.

BIRD a warm-blooded backboned animal with feathers. Most birds have wings.

BLUBBER a layer of fat which whales and some other sea *mammals* have around their bodies, and which helps keep them warm.

BROAD-LEAVED TREE a flowering tree with broad leaves, rather than the needlelike leaves of a *conifer*.

C

CAMOUFLAGE coloring or a pattern or a body shape that makes an animal hard to see in its natural surroundings. A speckled coat is good camouflage in a forest. White is camouflage in the snow.

CARIBOU a kind of large deer. This is the North American name for the animal known as reindeer in Europe.

CARNIVORE a meat-eating animal.

CLIMATE the kind of weather a place gets, for example, a desert has a dry climate and a tropical rain forest has a hot, damp climate.

COLD-BLOODED an animal which does not produce its own body heat. It depends on it surroundings for warmth.

CONIFER a tree with narrow, needlelike leaves. Most conifers produce their seeds in woody cones. A coniferous forest is a forest of conifers.

CORAL a tiny sea animal with a hard outer skeleton.

CRUSTACEAN an animal with a shell, belonging to the same group as crabs and lobsters.

CULTIVATE to grow plants especially for food, or to farm land so that food plants grow there.

D

DECAPOD an animal with a shell and which has five pairs of limbs used for walking. Crabs are decapods.

DECIDUOUS leaf-shedding. Deciduous trees shed leaves at the end of the growing season and sprout new ones when spring begins, or the rainy season starts.

DESERT an area of very dry land where few plants can grow and where, as a result, there are very few animals.

DINOSAUR a kind of prehistoric reptile that lived on land. Dinosaurs came in all shapes and sizes. The Age of the Dinosaurs started more than 200 million years ago and ended 65 million years ago, and was the time when dinosaurs were the most important backboned land animals.

DOMESTICATE to tame a wild animal and keep it and its descendants as pets or farm animals

DROUGHT a long period without rain.

E

EQUATOR an imaginary line around the middle of the Earth. The hottest parts of the world lie close to the equator.

EVERGREEN with green leaves all year round.

EVOLUTION the gradual process that gives rise to new kinds of animals or plants, over millions of years and many generations. By chance, one individual is born able to survive slightly better than others of its kind. Its descendants inherit that ability. Eventually, they give rise to a new kind of animal or plant. Meanwhile, the older, less successful kinds die out.

EVOLVE to change through the process of *evolution*.

F

FISH a swimming backboned animal with fins and gills.

FOOD CHAIN the link between eaters and what is eaten. Plants are eaten by some animals, those animals are eaten by other animals.

FOOD WEB animals eat more than one kind of food and are eaten by more than one kind of other animal. The criss-crossing of *food chains* form a food web.

G

GENE a tiny unit in the cell of a living thing. The genes in a young animal make sure it grows up like its parents.

GLAND a cell in the body of an animal or plant that gives out chemicals for the body to use. Some animals have scent glands, which give out strong scents.

H

HABITAT a place suitable for certain kinds of animals to live. For example, a tropical rainforest is one kind of habitat, a rocky seashore is another.

HERBIVORE a plant-eating animal

HIBERNATION an unconscious state some animals go into in cold weather. The heart slows down, the body temperature drops, and the animal stays in a kind of very deep sleep until warmer weather arrives in the spring.

HOME RANGE the area in which an individual animal lives and finds its food.

HUNTER-GATHERERS people who find their food by hunting other animals and gathering roots, leaves, and berries to eat. Early people lived this way and, in a few parts of the world, there are still people who live as hunter-gatherers.

I

ICE AGE a time when the Earth's *climate* is very cold and ice covers large parts of the north and south. There have been many Ice Ages.

INCISORS sharp teeth in the front of the animal's mouth.

INCUBATE to keep eggs warm until they hatch.

INSULATE to stop heat from escaping from something – feathers insulate a bird's body and keep it warm.

INVERTEBRATE a type of animal that has no backbone. Insects, spiders, shrimps, snails, jellyfish, and worms are just a few of the different kinds. There are many more invertebrates than there are animals with backbones.

L

LARVA the young of certain kinds of animals, such as many insects. Larva look quite different from the adult animals. Caterpillars, for example, are the larvae of butterflies and moths.

M

MAMMAL a type of backboned animal. Mammals are warm-blooded. They give birth to live young, which they feed with milk from their bodies.

MARSUPIAL a type of *mammal* that gives birth to its young while they are still very undeveloped and then usually keeps them in a pouch in its body until they are developed enough to move around on their own.

MIGRATE to travel from one area to another. For example, at the end of the summer, many birds migrate from the north to the south, where the weather is warmer and there will be more to eat.

MIGRATION the journey an animal traveler makes. See *migrate*.

MOLLUSK a type of *invertebrate* animal, usually with a shell. Snails are mollusks.

MUCUS slime that some animals, such as snails, have covering their bodies. Any slime produced by an animal's body is called mucus.

O

ORGANISM a living thing.

OXYGEN a kind of gas, found in the air. We need to breathe oxygen to stay alive.

P

PAMPAS the cool grasslands of South America.

PARASITE an animal or plant that lives on or in another animal or plant, getting the food it needs from that animal or plant.

PECTORAL FINS the fins at the front of the *fish's* body.

PELVIC FINS the fins at the back of *fish's* body.

PLACENTAL any *mammal* whose babies develop inside the mother's body, joined to the womb by means of a structure called a placenta. Placental *mammals* give birth to more developed young than *marsupials*.

PLANKTON water plants and animals that drift or float around. Some planktonic animals are the young (*larvae*) of much larger creatures, such as jellyfish.

POLES the imaginary points at the Earth's far north and south – the North Pole and the South Pole.

POLYP any small tube-shaped creature with one end fixed to something and the other with a mouth surrounded by *tentacles*.

PRAIRIE the North American grasslands.

PREDATOR an animal that hunts other animals for food.

R

REPTILE a type of *cold-blooded*, backboned animal, usually with scaly skin. Most reptiles live and lay eggs on land.

RODENT a type of *mammal* with chisellike gnawing teeth. Mice, squirrels, rats, beavers, and hamsters are all rodents.

RUMINANT a kind of *mammal* that eats plants, swallows its food and then brings it up again later as "cud", which it chews.

S

SAVANNA the hot grasslands of Africa.

SCAVENGER an animal that eats other animals, which are already dead when it finds them.

SPAWN the eggs of an animal which lives in or near water, such as frogs or *fish*.

SPECIES a distinct type of animal or plant that does not breed with any other kind.

STEPPE the grasslands of Central Europe and Asia.

SUCKLE the act of a mother *mammal* when she feeds her young with milk from her own body.

T

TAIGA the northern coniferous forest of Europe and Asia.

TEMPERATE a *climate* without very hot summers or very cold winters.

TENTACLE a part of an animal's body used for grasping or catching food. An octopus's "arms" are tentacles.

TERRITORY the area which an animal lives in and defends by driving away other creatures of the same kind.

THERAPSID a type of prehistoric *reptile* built rather like a *mammal*.

TIDE the daily rise and fall of the sea. This movement is mainly caused by the moon's gravity.

TRILOBITE a kind of early prehistoric animal that lived in water and had a shell.

TROPICS a region of the Earth which has warm, rainy *climate* all year.

TUNDRA land in the far north where the ground is frozen beneath the surface all year. Only low-growing plants such as mosses and tiny trees can survive.

V

VERTEBRATE any animal with a backbone. *Fish, amphibians, reptiles, birds,* and *mammals* are all vertebrates.

INDEX

ACKNOWLEDGEMENTS

Quarto Publishing would especially like to thank Heather Angel's picture library – Biofotos – for supplying the majority of pictures for this book. We would also like to express our grateful appreciation to the following picture libraries and photographers, for their help and patience in compiling this title:

Frank Lane Picture Agency; pgs. 17t, 18b, 20b, 21t, 23bl, 24bl, 24br, 27ct, 27br, 28b, 30tr, 30bl, 31tr, 31br, 38br, 39br, 40tl, 44cr, 48b, 59bl, 63br, 69tl, 69bl, 88tr, 90cr, 91bl. Survival Anglia; pgs. 10tl, 32c, 63bl. Eric & David Hosking; pgs. 19tr, 31tl, 38tr. Natural Science Photos; pgs. 39bl, 46br, 71bl, 83bl. C.M. Dixon; pg. 82. Finnish Tourist Board; pgs. 83cl. Ric Holland; pg. 83bl. Natural Image; pg. 86c. William S. Paton; pg. 86br.

While every effort has been made to trace and acknowledge all copyright holders, we would like to apologise should any omissions have been made.